DARK PSYCHOLOGY FOR BEGINNERS

2 Books in 1: How to Analyze and Read People Using Persuasion, Mind Control and Manipulation Techniques

Judith Dawson

TABLE OF CONTENTS

DARK PSYCHOLOGY FOR BEGINNERS
How to Analyze Anyone Through Mind Manipulation Techniques and Dark Psychology Tactics

MANIPULATION TECHNIQUES
Discover How to Analyze People Through Mind Manipulation, Psychological Techniques and Body Language

DARK PSYCHOLOGY FOR BEGINNERS

How to Analyze Anyone Through Mind Manipulation Techniques and Dark Psychology Tactics

Judith Dawson

CHAPTER 1
What Is Dark Psychology?

What is dark psychology, and how does it play a role in our lives? Dark psychology is the study of behaviors that coerce, influence, and manipulate other people (groups or individuals) for personal gain. It is a phenomenon that describes the psychological nature, behavior and methods behind, and how to use them effectively to persuade and control others. Dark psychology is well documented in extreme scenes such as criminal activity and mass manipulation in high control groups (in religion, business, and politics). These techniques are employed in everyday situations such as in sales, and in situations where subtle gestures and carefully chosen words can extend a deeper influence, which provides an advantage in getting what you want. Within the realm of dark psychology, many methods and techniques successfully give people the upper hand.

Understanding the Basics of Dark Psychology and its History in Research

Psychology has always been a fascinating area of study extending thousands of years, and other forms of science and philosophy. In recent years, the study of dark psychology became of growing interest and analysis. Many characteristics are associated with dark psychology. These behaviors are attributed to certain types of people and personalities who are more apt to manipulate. They use various techniques that involve the use of subtle, persuasive techniques or stronger tactics of control to achieve leadership, personal and romantic relationships, and other connections with people where there is the potential to gain more power. The study of dark psychology has focused on various personality types and professions, where the use of these techniques is more prevalent:

- Narcissism and sociopathy are often associated with dark psychology because people with these personalities use charm, a sense of importance over others (superiority), and the need to be adored and, or followed as a motive to manipulate others. Their lack of empathy and inability to feel remorse gives them a full range of tools to gain control in the most extreme ways in more skilled individuals, which can be done subtly and carefully over time. The techniques used by sociopaths and narcissists are often unethical, as they will often go beyond the tactics used by other people and have the potential to cause more harm.

- In politics, campaigns and speeches utilize influential language and emotion that captive people. Persuasive tactics can often drive people to vote for one candidate or party over another. Politicians and candidates are often good at convincing people that they will fulfill their promises if elected, which can be a powerful way to manipulate their decision on whether to support them or not.
- Motivational speakers are skilled at using dark psychology to captivate and heighten their audience's emotional reaction and dedication. They have a positive effect on behavior and action, while it can also promote merchandise such as books and products featured at the event as well. They have a way of making people feel as if they can achieve anything, and this creates a feel-good attitude where people are more open to suggestions to increase and prolong that experience.
- A successful sales associate convinces a potential customer or client of their need to buy or invest in a product or service. They may use motivational features in their tactics, and in some cases, evoke an emotional attachment or promise of better securing their future.
- Lawyers are skilled at winning their cases by using psychological tactics to get the results in their favor. This can be especially effective when the odds are not on their side, though they can shift the findings to support their client.

The techniques of dark psychology fulfill an agenda either intentionally through learned and developed ideas. These can be applied as unintentional methods that we may have picked up in childhood from our parents and family members, or at work, school, or in our immediate community. Aside from people who fit into the groups above, anyone willing to achieve their agenda through dark psychology can develop and use these powerful skills. You may know someone personally that uses dark psychological tactics to get what they want. They may be successful at it, and even if they are not always able to achieve everything, they are usually known for their talent for getting what they want. These individuals can be the source of envy because they are charismatic and easily persuade almost anyone to agree.

How Did the Study of Dark Psychology Begin?

The study of psychology is fascinating and has been for centuries. The study of the mind dates to ancient times when philosophers and critical thinkers took an interest in how we think, behave, and function. As technology and our understanding of the mind increased, specific areas of research became of interest, including the study of disorders related to mind, mood and thought, and many other ways in which we behave and respond based on our genetics and upbringing. Dark psychology began to evolve in the late 1800s, with the introduction of experimental psychology. Wilhelm Wundt, a scientist in Germany, was one of the first documented researchers of modern psychology, which also includes the analysis of philosophy and how we function in various environments and situations.

Wundt intended to study and record various sensations and thoughts in a way that connected our sensory and the mechanics of our brain. He noticed how certain chemicals were released and increased or lowered during certain events or incidents. Studies and their findings became the framework for mapping the mind and helping more people to understand the way we think and comprehend. During his career, Wilhelm Wundt trained almost 200 students to study psychology and work on furthering his studies for further understanding. While Wundt is considered the founder of psychology, his work set a standard that continues today, including a more specialized study into experimental and cognitive studies.

Where does dark psychology factor into the study of the mind? Specific areas of study included criminal psychology and other traits noticed in certain individuals, including people with "darker" personality characteristics, such as a lack of empathy and a tendency to manipulate. Dr. Robert Hare was known for his contribution to this fascinating field of study, which was referred to as "abnormal psychology." He developed several criteria and tests to determine the likelihood of someone with psychopathy and similar personality disorders or traits. While these studies focused on the dark side of the human mind, it is interesting to note that while a small portion of the population fits the criteria (about 3-5%), most people, at some point in life, have identified with the darker side or traits of humanity, even if momentarily. Not everyone possesses the capability of committing an unthinkable crime or losing all empathy towards other people. The darker side of the mind can occupy a bit of our thinking, even in the slightest ways, which can be undetectable. Consider some of the following examples that we can experience at any given time, despite having no signs of psychopathy or other personality disorder:

- A lack of remorse is a common trait in psychopaths. Most people experience empathy and feel regret when they do something wrong, especially if it impacts someone else negatively. While empathy can vary over time, it is lacking in individuals with an antisocial disorder. Consider, for example, when something awful happens to someone you deem deserving of the action. You may not feel the same sense of sadness or compassion for them. Consider if you had a hand in contributing to their downfall, even if it was justified, you may feel a sense of satisfaction or view the result as a form of justice or karma. For some people, this becomes exaggerated when they are not capable of feeling remorse or empathy, at least not to the degree as the average person. While most of us feel for others, there can be situations where this can fluctuate, depending on the circumstances and our involvement.

- Manipulation and persuasion are linked with darker personalities, including narcissism and psychopathy. In the most extreme cases, these characteristics are the foundation of a "dark" personality. However, for most people, developing the skill of persuasion, and to a degree, manipulation, can be of benefit and ensure their survival within various aspects of life, including their personal and professional livelihood. When we learn to use what we know to our advantage is a human trait that is practiced by most people, even if practiced to the detriment of someone else. How you sharpen your skills and improve your chances depends on how far you are willing to go, and well, you develop those traits.

- Charm and charisma are traits that are also associated with people who can easily manipulate and persuade other people. While these attributes do not automatically label a person as a psychopath or similar traits, they are easily used to attract other people who are viewed as conniving or

6

sneaky as they can persuade people into situations that they would otherwise refuse. A pleasant and outgoing personality can fit anyone, and some people are more friendly and receptive in certain circumstances than others. People who are naturally more charming can attract a crowd and become popular more easily. This method works well in the corporate world and politics, though it can be used in small communities or to gain favor with family, friends, and neighbors.

These examples of traits are shared by many people, not just the small portion of the population who are considered psychopathic or show signs of narcissism, though these characteristics are usually strong and more effectively used by them. By understanding dark psychology, there is much to gain from the types of methods to use in more practical situations where a nudge of persuasion or a dose of charm can give you the advantage. Despite the negativity associated with the dark side of the mind, there are useful tools and skills that you can use to improve your life in many ways, from work and community to home and family.

How to Begin Implementing Dark Psychology Techniques

Applying dark psychology may seem to require a lot of study and observation to pull off. While in more complicated or involving situations, more skill and practice is necessary to secure what you want, there are simpler modes of persuasion that work well under a variety of daily scenarios that many of us deal with. We have all been in situations where we need to take charge to prevent someone from taking control. It may be difficult to control the person(s) involved, though the circumstances surrounding the situation can be modified, sometimes quickly, to shift direction. Consider an incident where a colleague or client grows angry in reaction to what someone else says. The other person continues to inflate the friction by arguing further, trying to prove they are right or superior. While this can escalate into a much worse level of conflict, a third person or party can calm the situation by making a subtle yet validating comment. This can act as a "referee" moment between the two other parties and quell any further debate. While this isn't an example of dark psychology or manipulation, you can begin by making a calm, nonchalant comment to divert attention from a potentially explosive situation; the matter was quickly quieted and controlled. This method effectively "manipulates" the outcome to something more desirable.

Using simple, effective methods to manipulate a situation involves basic psychology. It's a good place to begin when learning the basics of dark psychology and how it can work for you. The following techniques don't require much effort, though they can significantly shape your environment and bend circumstances in your favor and give you the advantage at some point.

1. Smile and wave when you see someone you know or have seen before, even if you don't know them well. This will give them a good impression, if anything, that you are friendly and approachable. This works ideally in work environments where there are many employees, such as corporate offices or buildings. By making your mark this way, your positive attitude will stand out, and you may just run into this individual at a conference or work-related event that can enhance your networking and career-building ability. This method also works wonders if you are new to a specific neighborhood or community and want to make a good first impression without coming on too strong or pushy.

2. It's important to note that some people are easy to engage with once you get to know them. This includes bashful or shy people. Once they feel comfortable with a certain individual or group, they will open more about their thoughts and express more. When you make eye contact and take the time to hear someone, while nodding to affirm and validate what they say, this builds a stronger connection to an individual. Building a rapport will work in your favor later when you need them on your side.

3. Listening to music that you enjoy, just before a meeting or event that you wish to attend, can motivate, and prepare you to speak and behave with stronger confidence and a sense of purpose. Music is powerful and can uplift and strengthen your motive. This activity effectively "pumps" your mindset to a point where you feel stronger and more capable of addressing a crowd or a situation that can make you nervous initially. Some public speakers or performers boost their energy with music, motivational words, or affirmations for the same effect.

4. Keep positivity about you and other people consistent. This method will prevent you from developing a bad reputation in work and social circles. Avoid gossip, even if it seems benign

or harmless. Talking about other people often leads to saying something unflattering behind their backs. Once this information travels, it's hard to undo, even if it was a misunderstanding. Keeping drama out of your life is ideal. This simply means that some people do not want to communicate with you if they are gossip-centric, though you will gain more favor with other people who are ambitious and prefer to act instead of talk about it. Also, don't say too much about yourself, unless you don't mind it being repeated to others.

5. Keep in mind that you don't always have to respond. If someone makes an offensive or rude remark, you have the option to ignore it. When you respond, you give them the attention, and the outcome is usually an escalation to something worse. When you ignore them, even if this is difficult to do, the onus falls on them. This is a simple yet effective way to avoid conflict while forcing the other person to be held accountable for what they say.

6. Humor is a great way to break the ice, and it can also loosen any tension or bring down someone's guard. When you make someone laugh, they are less likely to gain the upper hand over you, and this gives you the advantage of turning the tables quickly. Laughter is enjoyable, so people tend not to mind, but it also makes them vulnerable and susceptible to the other person's intentions.

7. When you are in a situation where you are talking to someone who becomes too emotional, you can divert attention by mentioning facts involving numbers or dates. In some scenarios, you can ask them a question about a specific number, address, or date is the answer, and it may "pull" them out of their emotional state, even if temporarily. This technique can be applied in situations where people experience a traumatic event. In this situation, they may need to answer vital questions right away regarding a crime or other serious event. Often, they will forget important details later, though they may be able to recall a license plate or specific logo on a shirt immediately after an incident.

8. Use praise to give people a sense of credit, even if it's something minor, such as asking a question. We tend to be critical of ourselves, and often avoid asking a specific inquiry because it seems ridiculous. When we receive validation that the question

is good, or can provide more thought into a topic, this is reassuring and gives you a better platform to connect with them and build a rapport.

Many of the above techniques may be familiar to you, either because you've used them before or have experienced someone applying them when engaging with you. Chances are, you've had someone validate a question you asked at a seminar or conference, to make you feel less awkward or inhibited about the inquiry. When someone praises you for something, anything from fashion to an accomplishment, it feels good. Experiencing the above situations places us in a position of trust, at least partially, so that we are more apt to listen and follow what the other person wants us to hear. It's a tactic that you can use in response, to gain the same in return, or initiate during a conversation or initial interaction. The following techniques are also of benefit and often used to gain trust and confidence in someone, so they will provide a benefit or service in your favor. Some of these techniques may come easy to you, while others may require a bit of practice:

1. When you pose a question, sometimes the answer you receive is, "what?" It can be off-putting because it appears as though the other person didn't hear what you said, and you may be eager to repeat it. When this happens, it is more likely that the other person hasn't processed the question completely, nor have they been given enough time to absorb the information and respond differently. By allowing them that small space of time, you will appear less irritated, and the other person will feel satisfied to "recall" the inquiry on their own.

2. When directing an inquiry to a group of people, focus on one person at a time. The group may be collectively responsible, though they will usually delegate within to one or two people to handle each task or duty within a larger project. Paying attention to which people provide various details on specific aspects of a project or subject can give you a strong sense of which person(s) are taking on certain items. Once you follow this method and determine which person to direct your comment or question, it will give the group the sense that you are aware and paying attention. This option will leave a good first impression that is positive and builds confidence in what you know and how you engage. This

tactic is especially helpful in business and during job interviews with a panel or group.

3. People will give us an excuse when they're not interested in an offer, whether it's business or personal. It can be easy to take one direction or the other by responding with "that's ok" to affirm their lack of interest or to proceed with a rebuttal, which may result in reconsideration. While the first response does nothing to further your case, a rebuttal is not always helpful either. This can deter the person completely. The third option is to remain silent for a few seconds or longer, which will often prompt the other person to explain their reasons for saying "no." If their excuse is fabricated or untrue, they may eventually talk themselves into a corner and lose confidence in their response. You could have a second chance to offer again, and with more confidence than the other person.

4. When you encounter someone with an opposite view who wants to argue they are correct, it can be easy to assert your opinion or viewpoint over theirs to gain more credibility. This scenario has the opposite effect, and only causes the other person to feel more vindicated or reassured that they are correct. Instead, approach the response by validating what they say first, even if you do not agree or find their opinion offensive. You can state that "I see why you would think this way, because..." or "You have a valid point, and I respect that. Here is why I feel that..." Not only will the other person let their guard down a little and not feel so defensive, but they may also take a moment to listen to your point of view, even if you can't fully convince them they're wrong or incorrect.

5. One of the trickiest ways to gain information from someone or a company, when they are not permitted nor obliged to offer it, is to avoid vague questions like "who is the manager?" or "can you give me the phone number for ____?" This situation will allow the other person to explain that they cannot provide further details due to confidentiality. Instead, ask a specific question like "Is Dan still the manager here?" or "I have _____'s old cell phone number, can you tell me if it's correct?" This is a quick sleight-of-hand that can disable the other person's sense of protecting the information, and they may let their guard down, thinking

you may personally know the person or item that you're inquiring about.

6. The service industry is challenging, and it can make human interaction tricky when the customer or client is not cooperative. Clients can be especially challenging when they must wait for a product or service. When this happens, we are often inclined to apologize and state, "sorry for keeping you waiting" or "I apologize for the delay." While many companies require their employees to respond that they are sorry and take the onus for a business' shortfall, it is more effective to respond with "thank you for your patience," as this casually hints for their response to fall in line with showing forgiveness and patience. Often, the response will be "that's ok, it's not your fault" or "I understand you're busy, take your time.

CHAPTER 2
The Principles Of Dark Psychology

What are the principles of dark psychology? Dark psychology aims to employ useful tools and methods to control, manipulate, or persuade other people to gain an advantage. This field of study strives to understand and determine what mindset people have and how they put these techniques into action to control others. Understanding the principles of psychology is a major advantage in life because it helps us comprehend the human condition and how we use psychology to prey or target others for our benefit. In some cases, it's instinctual, while other forms of manipulation are purely intentional with an agenda or specific outcome. Dark psychology has been compared to criminal activity and psychopathic motives, though many people use various forms of these techniques to secure what they want in life.

Dark psychology embodies more than the far end of the spectrum that we often see depicted in films about serial killers and sociopaths. This refers to a category of mechanisms that are applied by many people to achieve what they want. Dark psychology also involves manipulating situations and/or people in their path to success. While forms of emotional and psychological abuse are linked to manipulation, many subtle yet impactful ways can give you a better chance of getting what you want, often with the other person unaware of what's happening. There are many aspects of dark psychology that spark controversy about how certain methods are used and their impact on other people; however, there is a positive component to using some tactics in circumstances where you can improve your chances of success. This book will show you how to use elements of dark psychology to your benefit, in both subtle and practical ways. These methods, when applied correctly, minimize the risk of failure while increasing the advantages of achieving your target or goal effectively.

Why Is Dark Psychology Effective and Why Do People Use It?

The techniques of dark psychology are powerful. They can exert undue influence over many people, including some individuals who are usually resistant to control or persuasion. People use dark psychology for many reasons. They develop and use various methods and techniques to achieve goals, both for ulterior motives and for broader gains for other people or groups as well. Persuasion is applied for many outcomes, including getting the next promotion, securing a job, or gaining favor within a social circle. Money, relationships, and improving social status are among the most common reasons for using dark psychology.

Dating, Sex, and Relationships

Charm and charisma are factors used to convince someone to engage in sex or begin a relationship quickly, often without the guarantee of commitment. This issue is not problematic where both parties engaging in intimacy have the same goals and are open about their intentions, whether there is a long-term commitment or not. Self-interest and immediate gratification are at the heart of using persuasion, and in some cases, more robust forms for manipulation, to convince someone to date or get involved romantically. There are many reasons why persuasion is useful at the beginning of a relationship and a way to engage in intimacy:

- Enjoying sex without commitment is thrilling and provides immediate gratification to the person who succeeds in seducing someone they are attracted to. In some cases, the idea of having sex is the only goal, and genuine chemistry is not needed.
- Do you relish the thought of pursuing someone, of chasing another person until they give in to your seduction? Seducing someone is a thrill or rush for some people, especially if it leads to mutual attraction. Sometimes the chase is more exciting for certain individuals, and the excitement falters once they get what (or who) they want.
- Securing a date and working towards a relationship with benefits, either sexual, social, or both, can be another reason to employ dark psychology methods. Even in cases where the other person feels a spark of attraction, it's not necessarily enough to secure dating and the possibility of a relationship without persuasion.

Doting on someone, giving compliments, and encouraging them to have a conversation with you can be done in both subtle and more direct ways. In some cases, a more candid approach works unexpectedly, and in other situations, a gentler manner brings success. You can gain a lot from a relationship, which can lead to better financial security, connections to social circles, and improving or establishing a reputation within that group and beyond. Self-interest is the reason in all cases, even if there is fair consideration given to the other person at times. Using dark psychology to seduce someone will always benefit the once pursuing that the one they want.

Why do people pursue relationships with dark psychology techniques? The reasons vary extensively from the desire for sex and immediate gratification to pursing specific kinks and fetishes while others aim to secure a romantic relationship for the long term to secure financial gain or improve their reputation. Persuasion is usually the best method to use when pursuing someone, as you'll want to ensure there is a chance they are interested in the same. There is also a level of transparency, which gives the other person an indication of your intentions, even if you choose not to disclose everything completely. For example, a person looking for sex without commitment may be straight-forward about it, though they may not disclose their desire to explore kinks and fetishes until they are involved with you intimately. Whether to disclose too much or too little in the beginning can make a significant impact on the outcome of a situation, because not everyone will want to know too much, or too little will leave them wanting to know more. For this reason, many people will focus on specific websites or groups that cater to their unique needs and desires, and while persuasion may still be used, they will have a better chance of getting what (and who) they want.

Dark Psychology in Politics

During campaigns and around election time, the prevalence of using manipulative and persuasive tactics are frequently used. Candidates use emotionally charged speeches and targeting their opponents negatively as part of a strategy to win. This can occur at all levels of government, from city or town councils to larger positions at a state or federal level. An elected official or politician will use similar tactics in their position, so they maintain their popularity and secure future success. Voters are heavily influenced by candidates in different ways, though essentially the outcome or goal is the same: they want to win, and the more votes and support, the better. What tactics convince citizens to support one candidate over another, and what techniques work?

- Taking credit and highlighting past triumphs and successes is a strong way to begin, as it builds confidence in the audience, and may appeal to undecided people. Claiming personal credit for situations when things are generally moving in a positive direction and shifting the blame of any poorly orchestrated decisions or ideas on the opposing parties or candidates is another tactic used regularly. Sponsored ads and supporters of one party or another often jump on board to claim their allegiance and utilize persuasive techniques of their own to gain attention for their own business or notoriety while supporting a specific politician or party at the same time.
- Some politicians are skilled public speakers and know how to frame or collectively group the status quo as something more positive than it is. This occurs once they secure a position in the office, and on the way, they will continually convince you that they are the solution to any problems that may arise. They may go as far as to blame opponents for being destructive and/or incompetent. This can be effective when there are major world events in action, and everyone is looking for something or someone to blame. It's an opportunistic time for candidates and politicians to position themselves as part of the solution and take credit for any progress, whether significant or small, to advance their popularity and credibility.

Many people may think they can see through political motives and tricks, and yet many of the same people will choose the same (or similar) candidates, despite signs that there is a manipulative nature at play. This is because political personalities appeal to a broad audience and often build their platforms on what people want the most while giving them a sense of hope if they are elected. Political strategies also apply at work and in community networks, where specific individuals use their popularity to propel themselves into positions of power and recognition.

Corporate and Business Strategies in Persuasion

Sales and the promotion of a business' products and services align with persuasion and manipulation, often on a more subconscious level. Most people who work in advertising or sales are aware of how promotional ads and campaigns aim to target specific people or demographics. This can be seen in the very nature of ads, and promotional campaigns, and how it works often goes unnoticed. When we take a closer, more scrutinizing look at how marketing works, we still may not see every fine detail used to sway our mind to buy and use a product or service. Some techniques are subtle, while others are more overt and obvious, and yet we are influenced either way.

In business, the persuasion and manipulation are often applied in positions of high stress and authority, whether it's a CEO making drastic restructuring changes to a corporation and must convince the other Directors to agree, or a sales associate looking to maximize their commission. In many situations, persuasion is a catalyst that makes an unattainable situation within reach. Strategies in business require a lot of communication, often to employees, clients, and/or stakeholders who may be anxious about the future of their company or line of business. Dark psychology often works its magic within these plans of action. These methods require creative "massaging" of words and the ability to relate to people on a human level, while simultaneously taking away something from them that will benefit you. The business world is brutal in this way because the bottom line always takes priority over everything and everyone else.

Forming Alliances in Business and Personal Situations

One of the most essential steps in starting a new job or joining a business is making a good impression and getting to know who you can trust and work with easily while avoiding difficult people and situations along the way. If you begin an entry-level job in a large corporation, the ability to climb the ladder to a better, more profitable position may seem like a stretch, unless you know how to network and stand out from your peers. One of the most important aspects of building a good network at your place of employment, or within a new community or upon joining an organization is to figure out simple attributes about the people you will work and socialize with:

- Who is easy to talk to and converse with, and who isn't approachable? You'll notice that the easiest people to talk to can offer a lot of information about the company and may even let you in on a few secrets if they like you.
- When meeting in a group, it can be difficult to determine which individuals like each other, especially if they all behave cordial and professional despite their differences.

When this happens, pay attention to individuals when they speak, and notice who they look at when they express themselves. It is human nature to look at someone who we generally like and agree with. This is especially the case when a strong statement is made, as the person presenting will seek visual confirmation from their "supporters" for a nod or show of approval as they speak.

- Follow their gaze and notice who they look towards, as this can give you a good idea of which people are in the same group or on the same "side."
- When you make a statement or present to the same group, focus on the same people with whom you know (or strongly suspect) will agree with you and support your direction. It is a powerful way to build an alliance with people you may not yet know because they can help give you the tools needed for the task and may benefit from it themselves. This is also a subtle act of persuasion.
- If someone else has a great idea, but they do not necessarily want to express it, take on the job for them. It can be a great way to give their idea merit and get some credit for helping them in the process. If you mention your idea originated from someone else, this can help give you more recognition for stating it. This is especially likely if you're accustomed to dealing with an employer or leader who doesn't focus on individual ideas but may take a collective brainstorm or referenced idea seriously.
- When you address a negative situation, de-escalating can be a challenging task. If you take the least confrontational approach, this can make it much easier to resolve. Imagine discovering a person in the process of stealing a few items from work, and you are the manager and would be held responsible for their actions. Instead of threatening them with disciplinary action right away, even when this may be imminent, you may be in a safer situation to advise them that there are cameras and motion sensors that could pick up on what they're doing. This takes the onus off you and makes them accountable. When the action must be reported, they will not necessarily hold you responsible, and management will commend you on handling the situation well.

Allying is not the difficult task it may seem to be and can be done using simple, easy-to-follow habits that can direct people to approach you more often, especially if you are willing to communicate new ideas and take notice of other people's actions. Being observant is one of the most important aspects of success and can make you stand out when you can recall or notice something that others dismiss. As you become acquainted with more people at work and how they behave with each other, you'll have a better sense of how to communicate with them and form strong connections that can give you a clearer path to what you want to achieve.

Ask for What you Want and Make it Count

What happens when we want a promotion or raise at work? We often hide behind smaller requests that may lead us in that direction eventually. When this happens, we miss out on the full benefit. Consider a situation where you want to ask for a raise, after working in the same position for over one year. Your performance reviews are satisfactory, and you're aware that the possibility of a pay raise or promotion is an option, but not a guarantee. In this situation, many employees stop short of asking for a raise and instead ask if there are any other positions or room to take on additional responsibilities, hoping this will automatically translate into a promotion and, or increase in pay. Often, this results in taking on more tasks with no definite raise in the future. Not only is this frustrating to take on more work with the same pay, but it also makes another statement to your employer: that you are willing to do more for less, and they may continue to take advantage of you for it.

Go big when you ask what you want at work. If you want a specific outcome, ask if the question you are ready to pose will bring it about, or if it's merely a distraction from what you can have now. There are a few reasons why we don't boldly ask for what we truly want, including the following:

- We assume that what we truly want is out of the question and that we won't get it. This situation happens because some employers give their staff the impression that they should be grateful for their job, especially when the economy is slow. Inadvertently, this gives employees the idea that they should be happy to work and not pursue any further pay or promotional options until a much later time.

- Be direct and don't feel ashamed to ask for what you want, even if it seems trivial. Sometimes a small favor granted can hint towards something much more substantial later on. You may need to establish that you'll get a little of what you want now in preparation for bigger ambition in the future.

Strategies for Manipulation in Advertising

Consider some of the reasons we are apt to pay attention to some ads more than others, and the techniques that influence us. It is no mistake that certain jingles or slogans ring in our minds for a prolonged period, while certain images are branded into our memory to continuously remind us of a specific restaurant, brand, or product. Among all the effective strategies used for advertising, the most effective are subliminal because they awaken our subconsciousness and make a lasting impression. By the time we realize how effective or memorable an ad is, we've already been impacted by it long ago. Consider the following techniques that not only convince you to buy a service or product. The next time you notice a billboard or banner across your television or computer screen, think about some of the following attributes and how they impact and connect with you on a personal level:

- The placement of objects or images is an over-looked technique that works to manipulate our mind into processing what we observe differently. For example, placing an image on the left side of a screen or advertisement will increase the fluency or speed at which we process, often resulting in a positive reaction or impression. How often do we notice the placement of objects on a screen or billboard? It likely never crosses our mind, and yet it has a subconscious effect on how well we receive the overall message.
- Placing objects on the left-side and from certain angles can also produce a more favorable impression of the object itself and the message. If the ad features a specific product or service in this way, you are more drawn to it positively. Some studies indicate that adding a person or other objects are held or being used, the favorable effect of placing the object on the left is less effective.
- When you add a utensil or tool to another object, to showcase its use is value, this placement and state of utility makes an impact. Generally, people want to see a product

in a state where they can relate to using it, such as butter on a slice of bread, instead of displaying a loaf of bread in a bag or placing a spoon or fork in a mouth-watering bowl of soup or cereal. Shoes, clothing, and accessories are best shown with their laces or openings (zippers, buttons) obvious, so they appear functional and practical. In all these instances, people can relate to using these products and would be more apt to buy them.

- The size of lettering or text has a profound effect on how people perceive an ad or message. Studies conducted on merely increasing the size of words and messages showed a direct impact on the emotional response of the audience. Generally, the larger the font or lettering, the more impactful the message. This effect is magnified when a specific word or phrase in a sentence is bolded or enlarged more than the remaining words or letters. This is a powerful way to evoke an emotional response and is often used in fundraising or awareness campaigns, but also in the marketing of products, often to align them with providing a benefit to satisfy an emotional want or desire.

- When luxury products or services are promoted, strong and assertive language is best for successful persuasion. Those of us who are drawn to exclusive services, and merchandise related to the sense of importance and urgency, to try the next and newest product of pleasure. For most ads, the idea of using a more aggressive tone is avoided because people generally do not like feeling as if you're trying to persuade them, hence the subconscious and subtle tactics that are often used. For luxury or specialized services that appeal to a more hedonistic or pleasure-seeking audience, this is an exception.

- Using similar words or rhyming, even using a small or short poem, can have a favorable effect on people. When a slogan is balked at as silly or juvenile, it still grabs people's attention, and it stays with them, despite the initial negative reaction. Slogans and jingles that rhyme or have a catchy set of words that sound similar are hard to forget. You may remember specific commercials and ads from your childhood solely because of a specific line or phrase that was unique. This is the genius behind advertising and its effects in both the short and long-term. Consider the following examples:

- o "Do you want something more? Shop at our store!"
- o "You deserve the best. Shop with us, we'll take care of the rest."

- As previously stated, images on the left side of an ad have the effect of being processed quickly and more positively, though if an image is large and intricate, it may work best positioned on the right side. This is because of how our brain processes visuals. If you place your product on the left, the logo will be more effective on the right.

- The size of your product or brand makes a difference, and it increases the persuasion factor. You can persuade potential customers to try your brand without overtly saying it. In some cases, it is advised that reducing the size of the product is best if it is given a center stage or highlighted on a page or ad with a border or graphics. Generally, increasing the size of a product is optimal for getting the attention you want for marketing.

- In addition to the font size and lettering, the color and design make an impact as well. Other attributes that also leave an impression include spacing, the positioning of the letters, and the line or font style. If you want to showcase your brand as fancy or decorative, you may want to use a cursive font, though this may not attract the attention if they are difficult to read or blend in with the background or image. For impact, lettering must be like a label: it should stand out and vary enough in color and style to be seen without difficulty.

- Ads or campaigns that promote beauty and wellness products often use angular designs and long, slender lines and strokes in their font. This gives the concept of beauty because these styles are easy to read and considered visually pleasant. Placing objects or graphics on the left side of an ad has the benefit of being processed quickly and seen as favorable and beautiful at the same time. Thin lines in font, even if a standard style is used, make a better impression than a thick, bolded style.

- Designing a unique logo or style of writing is another way to connect with people, as they will always remember your products or service when they spot your logo or any related style. From childhood, many of us can recall at least one restaurant or store from an old logo, even if it has been out of circulation for many years. Product designing follows the same principle. Color coordination and lettering goes a long way to securing a familiarity and planting a firm impression in your mind that will last for months, years, or possibly a lifetime.

- Color is impactful for many reasons. In business, many people wear specific colors or styles to convey a sense of authority or, at the very least, to get your attention and keep you engaged. This works in advertising by giving the audience a sense of urgency: red and yellow are typically used for ads that say "stop" or "caution" before introducing you to a new home security system or safety equipment. The cautionary approach appeals to many people when they are concerned about their security and safety. Cooler colors such as blue and green are best for ads that convey a service that is meant to calm or soothe, whereas red, orange, or yellow give you a greater sense of urgency to act to solve your problems right away. As effective as color can be in advertising, it can clutter or blur the overall message, which can be counter-effective. In these ads, only a part of the message, usually the wording and one or two items in the picture stand out as bright or colorful, while the remainder of the ad is pastel or faded.
- People or model placement in ads create the face of the product, and often with a positive reaction or smile. This effect gives the audience a good impression of the usefulness of the brand and its appearance.

One major characteristic of advertising is to make an appeal to a specific demographic and evoke an emotional response. We may not always notice how we react to an ad until later when it creeps into our mind about a personal experience or feeling. This effect can be triggered later in subsequent advertising campaigns, especially when a certain brand or product has staying power and continues to foster a relationship with us. Traditional products will often rebrand and re-package to appeal to a changing generation. A slogan or message may be added to a service or product to align a company or brand in support of current events and movements in the news. This has the effect of gaining new customers and can create a strong and powerful emotional attachment. Some people will attach their loyalty to a specific brand or company because of their political stance or ethical practices. A brand or company that does not adapt to current situations becomes an "endangered species" in business and risks loss as a result.

Framing is an effective tool that takes a negative or positive situation, such as a medical condition or common inconvenience, and markets a solution in the form of a product or service. Pharmaceutical ads are notorious for promoting a solution to almost any medical problem. They must follow strict guidelines for marketing, including the disclosure of side effects, though feature family-friendly themes that align with our desire to feel comfort and relief from pain, often caused by many chronic health conditions they promote treatment for. Negative framing refers to using a concern or fear we have about life, whether it's a pandemic or a concern about rising crime in a neighborhood, to market security products or protective equipment to give us a sense of improved security. When framing is negative, it is most likely to create an urgent need to react quickly, which is often the case and can trigger a high volume of success within a short time. This is effective when done in a time-sensitive manner to address current events and concerns of today.

Positive framing is a way to generate curiosity and interest in a product that you may never consider before. When a problem is posed and a solution offered, the positive frame conjures excitement about a new product or service with statements such as "see what we can do to improve your success today" or "improve your stamina and brain health with our revolutionary brand..." Even the most skeptical reader will take a closer look to find out more about the buzz or trend. This method is a slight, but powerful way to grab anyone's attention and persuade them to peek, if not outright purchase your product.

Inclusivity is a major topic of conversation in many aspects and is often involved in many discussions from socioeconomic to political topics. Advertising has also picked up on the importance of showcasing diversity in their ads and slogans, and as many companies shift their focus on including more samples of society, including models with "real" body types and people from all ages, backgrounds, and ethnicities, the target audience continuously expands and engages more people today. Gone are the days of traditional roles from decades ago. Advertising is overtly more inclusive with images and how products once marketed to one group are now branded for everybody, from cars and personal computers to beauty products. Featuring "real people" in ads has had a major impact on improving the way people feel about the products in these ads, giving the advertiser or company the advantage.

What Methods Applied in Dark Psychology

There are simple yet effective techniques that are used to gain favor and control in one-on-one conversations, which can evolve into more complex systems of observation and knowing which people to "target" or focus on to employ those methods. Some specific techniques and practices are natural for some people to develop on their own, while others will practice and train their behavior to become more effective in their ability to influence and gain power.

The Basic Concept of NLP or Neuro-Linguistic Programming

Neuro-linguistic programming or NLP is a practice that is used by many professions that entails observation of physical and verbal cues in other people and using techniques to understand and influence them. NLP has been used in many professions since its development almost half a century ago, and while it has been the source of controversy and debate on its effectiveness, the practices are still widely used today. More details on the specific techniques and how they are used are featured in chapters 4 and 5.

Hypnosis

A powerful and often overlooked method, the practice of hypnosis grew in popularity in the 1700s and has steadily become more common in its use ever since. Hypnosis is defined as a practice that regulates consciousness in a way that can control, and in some cases, supersede certain forms of behavior and perception. Despite arguments against its use or effectiveness, hypnosis is used today to treat many conditions such as addiction, trauma, and behavior control. It's widely applied for a variety of reasons and treatments, many of which people find helpful in life. Therapists will conduct hypnosis to understand underlying reasons deep within their patients, which often include resurfacing past experiences, including traumatic events.

How effective is hypnosis? Some individuals are more open to suggestion and influence than others, which means the results vary. The more influential the person, the more likely you will be able to induce a state of hypnosis and exert more control over their thoughts and actions. In this state, the mind is easily persuaded with less effort than in our regular conscious state. You can instruct a person to recall painful or difficult memories more readily in this state, as a means to understand their emotions and thoughts during the process. These methods are often used in therapy, though there are other instances when hypnosis is used, such as live stage performances, where members of the audience volunteer to be induced into a state of hypnosis for entertainment purposes.

One of the most controversial aspects of hypnosis has always been its intention and how it is applied. In scientific research and for therapeutic reasons, it can provide a window into the mind for further understanding of how our mind and cognitive process works. Some studies have indicated an improvement in memory when hypnoanalysis is applied, though there have been reports of false or distorted memories that have had a traumatic impact on people. When used in the context of entertainment for shock value or as a means to gain power or control over another person without their knowledge, it can be a subject of debate as to whether it should be used at all.

When is hypnosis used to persuade and guide someone towards a favorable decision or to fulfill an ulterior motive? The power of this practice is in the hands of the person inducing the state in their target, whether it's to relieve them of a medical condition or psychological trauma or to induce a state in which they can use their power to influence and "trick" the other person to see and behave differently. Hypnosis is more than controlling what the other persons see and remember; it can alter their current perception, behavior, and can be used as a tool to mold their actions. The techniques used in hypnosis are often subtle, but effective, much like the subliminal messages we see, but may not overtly notice, in magazine, television, or online ads.

How Hypnosis Works

To induce a state of hypnosis, a certified hypnotist will use various cues or suggestions to shift your consciousness into a trace. This can be done with the repetition of words or sounds that gradually bring about this state. Once this is achieved, the patient or other person experiences a daydreaming-like state. They may feel as though they are in a dream and not fully conscious. Hypnosis works like NLP as it shifts a person into an altered state of consciousness by using verbal cues along with repetition. Certain forms of music or consistent rhythms have been known to induce similar states of various consciousness, which are often seen as euphoric or "high." During this state, a person is more likely to follow instructions and focus on an object or concept, whereas in a normal state of consciousness, they would usually ignore or dismiss it. This position gives the hypnotist the advantage because they now can use suggestions to evoke certain actions and behaviors that would otherwise not be possible.

Inducing an Altered State of Consciousness for Greater Influence and Persuasion

How can you use hypnosis to your advantage? You don't have to be a certified hypnotist to take advantage of the techniques used in this process. Often, we are subjected to variations of hypnotic influences or may notice someone else's guard is let down, and they are more receptive to suggestions or ideas when they are under the influence of alcohol or other substances that loosen their inhibitions. This state can be brought about by other means in various settings. Consider the following situations and how they can alter a person's ability to fall under a more suggestive or agreeable state:

- A live concert or music event with loud, rhythmic, and repetitive beats can induce a trance-like state in some people, where they are more likely to give in to someone and let their guard down. Have you ever approached a person at a club or venue and found them far more agreeable and perceptive to you than at work or in another place without the same stimuli? This could be due to being under the influence of alcohol as well, though the rhythmic nature of music can have a hypnotic effect on some people.
- Meditation and some forms of yoga have been used to reach a different level of consciousness. Some people find they are more receptive when they are in a meditative state. Self-hypnosis is another way in which people can induce a more suggestive state within themselves, which can also influence others around them if done in a group setting. This can have a profound effect on influencing more than one person at a time.

- Certain drugs or hallucinogens can induce various states in which you are conscious and focused, but also more likely to bend to someone else's suggestions and less hesitant in general.
- Some websites or television shows may feature a segment with moving objects or flow or design, rotating with consistency that brings about a hypnotic state or trance. This isn't always noticeable, and may only last momentarily, though it is also a common tool used in advertising or gaming apps to keep players and consumers engaged for hours at a time.

While there are many obvious ways in which we can be swayed to purchase a product or service or follow a trend or group, there are many subtle ways that we notice every day, from the patterns or colors used in ads on billboards to banners that rhythmically dance across your computer screen in the middle of an online conversation or while playing a game. When asked how much we see in advertising and are influenced daily, we likely only recall a fraction from our consciousness, while our subconscious retains far more, and has a strong impact on our spending and lifestyle decisions, despite thinking that our choices are completely our own.

CHAPTER 3
Learning How To Use Techniques Of Persuasion And Manipulation

Understanding the various traits of dark psychology can give you an advantage in many situations. Taking a look into each of these characteristics will give you a better idea of what it means to be persuasive versus manipulative, and how a dose of charisma and paying closer attention to the next person you meet can take you much further than expected.

The Difference Between Persuasion and Manipulation

Many people use these terms interchangeably, though they are distinctly different in their definition and purpose. The technique or method used depends on the specific situation and the circumstances of the person. Persuasion is often viewed as a gentler form of manipulation that focuses and builds on the general intention of another person. The desire to persuade someone else can be a way to encourage them to pursue or accomplish a task that they are considering, though they may feel doubtful about their abilities or the outcome. In this way, you are applying pressure or encouragement to secure their decision in a specific direction. They are already considering this as an option, and the act of persuasion will give them the needed "push." Manipulation, on the other hand, conceals your true intention and aims to convince the other person that there is a benefit for them (or mutually) when the result is an advantage to you. This requires stronger tactics, which increase with severity when the other person is resistant to deciding in your favor. In reviewing the differences between persuasion and manipulation, it's clear how each tactic has its advantages in specific situations.

Persuasion

- There is transparency in the process of persuasion, without a hidden agenda or deceit, because both parties are aware of the desire to sway the other person towards a decision.

- The other person is considering the proposal and simply hasn't finalized their decision yet. This can be a mutually beneficial move if they stand to benefit in some way from the persuasion, and all they need is that extra reason or confirmation to proceed.

- Persuasion can be a selfless act when the other person stands to benefit more than anyone else. For example, you may convince someone to apply for employment in a progressive company, even if they don't feel they are qualified, though may try if they are convinced that their resume and credentials are worth consideration.

Manipulation

- The act of manipulation requires concealing your true intentions to sway the other person's mind into a decision that will provide more of a benefit for you than them. This would imply taking someone into making an expensive purchase to benefit your sales commission, even when it is clear that this is not the most feasible decision for them.
- There is little or no transparency in manipulation. There is always a hidden agenda so that the other person is not always aware of their lack of benefit and what you stand to gain from it. Even when they become aware of this, further manipulation, if skillfully done, can convince them enough that there is something in it for them.
- Conjuring a sense of urgency or fear and using emotional expressions can go a long way to convince someone to decide that they would otherwise never consider.

Both manipulation and persuasion have the same goal, though the underlying tactics and reasons for using both methods vary considerably. The degree to which you use persuasion depends on your specific circumstance, and whether manipulation is needed to take a stronger approach towards securing what you need. For example, closing a sale may begin with a persuasive technique, as you convince the potential buyer that they need the product. When they refuse, you may increase the pressure by noting there is a sale that ends within a day or that the product(s) will only be available for a limited time, and not making the purchase will forfeit any future benefits. Sometimes this tactic, as harsh as it may seem, can effectively "push" someone to sign a contract on the spot, to avoid missing the sale, or spend more than they initially anticipated.

Understanding the Importance of Developing Good Persuasion Skills

The most skillful manipulators begin as masters in the art of persuasion. They have developed the abilities to observe and determine the other person (their intended target) and what it will take to convince them to decide or move in a specific direction. Persuasion is an effective set of skills that can help anyone from business leaders and CEOs to everyday situations working in retail or sales positions. It's an important set of techniques to apply in your personal life when dealing with indecisive people or difficult scenes that need someone with the ability to nudge and direct an individual or group of people in the right direction. You may already use persuasion skills in life without knowing it, as it is a practice many of us learn in childhood, such as convincing a parent to buy ice cream or go to the local park or fairgrounds. It's a habit many of us have learned at a young age, though as we grow older, we adapt our communication into adulthood. Further development of persuasion techniques can be done by using what we already have while applying new ways that work well in a variety of situations.

What Are Your Strengths? Use Them to Your Advantage

Are you good reading people or finding something in common with a coworker or new acquaintance? You may be an excellent conversation starter or know the right time to say specific words or phrases when they will have their desired impact. All these attributes and more can make your persuasion very effective and successful.

Point of View from Another Perspective

One of the items lacking in many attempts to persuade or convince someone is not being able to see their point of view. This is the myopic or short-sighted view and can dismantle any chance you have in convincing someone. It not only limits your ability to make a meaningful connection with the other person, but it also increases the chances that they will see you as inflexible and lacking compassion unless you can demonstrate an appreciation or understanding of their side or viewpoint. Making this connection bridges a lot of gaps that many people have, though do not often see a work-around when trying to reconcile, then make their case.

Persuasion becomes far more effective when the other person is convinced that you understand and acknowledge them.

Expect Arguments and Prepare for Them

Some persuasive techniques are not won without a battle, and for this reason, you must plan for the likelihood that you'll encounter resistance. Most people are not as indecisive as they may appear, and any attempt to sway their opinion or decision in another direction can be met with a fight. Consider this a possibility for all situations and prepare what you will say in response to them. A counter-argument should be done respectfully, and listening to the other person, despite how much you may disagree or dislike what they have to say, is important for framing your next move and how you will proceed.

Become a Problem Solver

This requires good listening skills and determining which obstacles the other person has that can prevent them from being convinced. For example, if a person doesn't have the money to start a small investment fund or make little contributions each month, you can offer a free evaluation of their budget for ideas. This can help them "find" a way to fit a weekly or monthly contribution to make. Instead of explaining all of your reasons to convince or persuade someone first, allow them to state their opinions and concerns. Not only will this make your job easier in persuading them which product or option is best for them, but you'll also have a more captivated audience because you listened and acknowledged them first.

There is Always Common Ground

We often see each other's differences before we share what we have in common with others. This often leads to misunderstanding and using words or terms that may not connect with others. For example, if you find that another person enjoys live theatre, you can relate to them by asking about their favorite productions, then drawing them into a conversation to persuade. If the specific item that you have in common with them relates to part of the persuasion or decision you wish to sway them towards, then you are at a great advantage.

Show Confidence and Don't Be Afraid to Show It

Many people who are not too difficult to persuade may become deterred if they see a hint of hesitation or uncertainty in your tone of voice or body language. Being confident in what you have to say and what you want to convince them to do is a major step towards securing success. People sense confidence. For this reason, practice your speech and what you want to say, and make sure your voice is assertive and strong. The more practice, the easier it will be to make an impactful impression that instills confidence in the other person.

Using Body Language That "Mirrors" the Other Person

This technique may seem subtle, but its effect is powerful in appealing to other people. Mirroring is used when you notice a shift in body weight or slight gesturing or posture changes that you observe in someone, then copy them in a way that is not too obvious. If someone is speaking in a soft tone and is gentle in their speech, it is advantageous to bring your tone of voice into the same realm, as this will give them the impression that you are meeting them on the same level. A stronger tone or voice or more blunt approach may be required if it is used and expected by the other person, though do so carefully, and observe whether it is having a positive impact on connecting with them. Mirroring gives the other person the impression that you are following their lead and letting them control the direction of the conversation, even as you successfully apply persuasion techniques.

Make Notes and Remember Key Information

Taking notes during a conversation, especially in business or professional situations, may seem unusual if you are not used to this practice. Taking notes is a good idea for a few reasons:
- You don't have to remember every detail of the conversation, and making notes will capture the most vital points that you can refer to later, while in the same conversation or at a later time.
- Taking notes shows interest in what the other person has to say. They will notice this as a positive and may divulge more information as a result, knowing they will be heard and recorded.

- This will build confidence in the other person, and they will trust that you can use this information to advise or provide useful information.

Learn and Use People's Names

When a person hears their name, they not only enjoy the personal touch of the communication, but appreciate that you remember who they are, and are more likely to respond favorably. Using their name in a conversation more than once, though not excessively, is a way to let them know that you are considering them personally, which has a positive reaction.

Never Give Up and Be Persistent

Persistence pays off, though it is often avoided or overlooked as too aggressive of an approach or unlikely to work. On the contrary, carefully timed and consistent persistence in following up with people can make a major impact on how likely they are to change their minds or finalize a decision. This is especially important in situations where the other person is not sure what to decide and asks for time to think it over. This is a prime chance to reach out to them. Take into consideration any connection you made on your initial meeting and use this to your advantage to secure a working relationship with them. Your contact with them could be the catalyst that secures their decision in your favor.

Research Ahead and Prepare

Know your target and aim with precision. This can only be done when you know what you're talking about and get to know who you are talking to. The more you understand the person and their needs, the more you can appeal to them on this level. They will listen to you more intently and on a personal level if you appeal to them on a deeper level. For example, if someone owns a small business or is employed in a specific field of work, this may give you the advantage of connecting with them. You may use this information to convince them that a specific service or product is right for them.

The Basics of Manipulation and How it Compares and Evolves From Persuasion

Manipulation is a much stronger form of persuasion that aims to get you what you want, regardless of the outcome of the other person. When you make the shift from using persuasive techniques to more manipulative tactics, there are some key points to consider. Persuasion is often the first way to influence other people, especially if the task involves "pushing" or convincing them to move or continue in a specific direction or decision. Manipulation is a stronger method that requires more control over the other person, which is often done when the other person is on track towards moving in the opposite direction of where you want them to go. At this point, you will need stronger tactics to change their mind. You'll need to convince them with more powerful tactics, which can lead to making them feel a sense of duty or commitment to you or an organization, which can "guilt" them into working in your favor or using fear or a sense of obligation to secure the same result.

When do you cross the line from persuasion to manipulation, and how can this be done effectively?

- It's important to know the other person, their needs, and their desires. They may say "no," and while this may be their true response, pay attention to hesitation and whether they are still thinking internally, even if they appear definite in their decision. This can leave a slight opening of opportunity to convince them to say "yes" with points and ideas that can appeal to them.
- Convincing someone that you know what they want, even better than they do, can take some practice and skill. In this way, you play the expert, and with confidence and knowledge, this can be pulled off. It is a form of manipulation that gives them the impression that you can figure them out and understand their needs well, even better then they can, to gain their confidence in you. For example, you may be turned down when offering a service to a small business, though by knowing the history and financial struggles of the company, you can gain their trust by convincing them that what you have to offer will increase their income and success. Relating to them on a personal level and appealing to their need for improved business can be the breaking point that convinces them to switch in your favor.

Persuasion or Manipulation? Learning the Differences Between Them and How They Can Be Effectively Applied to Your Benefit in Various Case Scenarios

As described earlier in this chapter, persuasion and manipulation are similar in some ways, with distinctive differences in how they are used to get what you want. Persuasion is the best skill set when the other person is on their way to deciding and needs a stronger sense of guidance. They need a final push or nudge to change the "maybe" or "I think so" to a definite "yes." Manipulation can change a "no" or "I don't think so" into a "yes."

How do persuasion and manipulation techniques work in real case scenarios that we face daily? Often, we don't realize how many opportunities there are to convince someone in our favor, and we can miss this chance by not effectively observing their behavior and planning effectively what to do next. How does this play out in situations at work, in the office or showroom, or personal relationships?

Scenario 1: The Sales Associate

Sonia was hired as a sales associate for a high-end furniture store. The showroom was well organized to display a wide range of good quality products at a premium price. During the first week, except for a few small orders, Sonia failed to close on any big sales. She was given a month to prove her ability, and during this time, she decided to study various techniques in both persuasion and manipulation that could move her closer to meeting her targets. In the second week, she met with a family who was interested in a new dining room set. The specific set they were considering was one of the most expensive models and would be enough to establish confidence with Sonia's boss if she made the sale.

Brenda, the wife of Greg and mother of two preteen kids, was keen on the prestigious dining room set, despite her husband's hesitation. He was worried about the budget and whether they could afford it. Brenda assured Greg they had the money and deserved to splurge on themselves. Sonia faced a dilemma: she could stand by and watch them decide on their own, taking a passive stance, or she could appeal to the emotional needs of Brenda, who wanted to invest in their new home. The kids appeared bored and wandered around the store, leaving the parents to argue about the decision to buy the table and chairs. During this time, Sonia had a chance to consider how to appeal to them by observing and learning the following:

- They could afford the dining room set, but Greg was convinced it was not a good buy, while Brenda wanted to enhance the appearance of their home. She saw the purchase as an investment, while he viewed it as a burden.

- Both kids were old enough to be in junior high or secondary school, which meant they likely had homework to do every week. The dining room table would provide a communal space for both kids and their parents to work together, as needed.
- A good quality dining room table and chairs would last longer, provide a better warranty, and in general, more cost-effective for a family. This would make a better impression on guests and extended family, especially over the holidays.
- Any concerns about paying for the furniture all at once could be easily handled through a financing plan.
- Both parents worked full-time, though finances were tight due to some extra, unexpected expenses over the past couple of months.

Sonia prepared to offer the family a good financing plan with a reasonable interest rate while deferring the first two payments without interest. They would not require a down payment, and they could order the set and have it delivered within a week. During the holiday season, which was just two months away, having a new dining room set would be a nice "gift to themselves," Sonia suggested. The idea of treating themselves lit up Greg's face, as he realized they had been working so hard, and coming home to a sleek, comfortable seating arrangement where they could enjoy home-cooked meals as a family was a worthwhile investment. When Greg hesitated to sign the offer, Sonia politely reminded him that he was doing this for his family, and they would all thank him for it later. With that statement, the sale was made, and Sonia was on her way to make the first of many more sales in the furniture store.

What methods did Sonia use to convince both Brenda and Greg to buy the furniture? In the beginning, she already had Brenda's "buy-in," which was in her favor. Brenda didn't require much persuasion to buy the dining room set, as her mind was already made up; however, Greg was opposed to it and suggested a less expensive option instead. This disagreement between the couple could have easily led to Brenda accepting Greg's option until Sonia stepped in to convince them to take it. Persuasion was the primary technique because while Greg was leaning towards a "no," he was generally on the fence and willing to move towards his wife's suggestion with a bit of convincing. If Greg was able to convince Brenda that another option was better for their family, Sonia would have to use stronger, more manipulative techniques to sway their decision back towards the original dining set.

Scenario 2: Making a Date

Todd was charismatic and good looking, which was an easy way to gain favor and make a positive impression on most people. He was successful in business and worked in marketing, which allowed him to meet many new people regularly. Most women he encountered enjoyed his company, and his charm won him many dates and a few intimate relationships over several years. On one occasion, Todd met Dana, who was friendly, attractive, and very savvy in her line of business. They met at a conference, and Dana was easily swept into a conversation by Todd, who was eager to get to know her more. Not only was he attracted to her romantically, he observed how well people gravitated towards her, and how this would benefit him to be in her presence. Securing a relationship with Dana would mean a lot to gain, in business and his personal life.

After meeting for the second time at another business conference, Todd entertained the idea of asking Dana on a date. He made it sound playful, not as serious as if they were just grabbing dinner with the possibility of a drink. Dana hesitated before mentioning that she was unavailable. Todd nodded and smiled as if to accept her response, though he decided to find out more about Dana, in case it would help him gain her favor and possibly convince her to trust him enough for a date. It was easy at first; Todd retrieved a business card from Dana and did some digging online into her line of work, which involved event planning. He learned that she wasn't married. She was popular with a lot of people and seemed to take an interest in antiques and road trips, according to her professional social media profile. Dana's credentials were impressive, and she liked to travel extensively. This gave Todd some information for the next time they would meet.

A month later, Todd met with a few colleagues for lunch. He conveniently chose (and suggested) a café when he unexpectedly bumped into Dana. Todd knew there was a slight chance that Dana might be in the area since she had mentioned some nearby shops and businesses briefly during a previous conversation. Their conversation was more relaxed than usual, and Todd invited her to join him for coffee after lunch, which Dana readily accepted. During the two hours they spent together, Todd casually mentioned his enjoyment of old architecture and specifically interior décor that resembled turn-of-the-century designs. This resonated with Dana, and he knew she enjoyed antiques, which made it easy to find common ground. Todd also mentioned that he was considering taking a drive out of town to explore a few small towns at some point over the summer, which piqued Dana's interest as well since she was a fan of road trips. During their exchange, Todd was careful to observe Dana's gestures and mannerisms, which indicated that she was more eager to get to know him and potentially agree to a date. Instead of pursuing the question to date, Todd offered his business card and nonchalantly asked Dana to give him a call if she wanted to join him on his road trip. She accepted the card, and a day later, she called to ask more about his drive out of town. Todd acted vaguely at first, which encouraged Dana to explain more of her love of travel and antiques. Furthermore, she unleashed a lot more about her personal life and struggles, which made her successful today. She would soon be ready to accept the invitation to dinner, Todd thought, and shortly thereafter, Dana agreed to meet for drinks and dinner at a local restaurant. Their meeting quickly evolved into a working relationship where Todd gained more knowledge about Dana, and how her expertise could help him gain access to more business connections and opportunities than before.

What tactics did Todd use, and were they persuasive or manipulative? Initially, Todd appeared straight-forward in his approach to ask Dana on a date, and while he did find her attractive, his primary motive was to secure a better networking strategy to further his agenda and secure more contracts. Dana did enjoy Todd and his company, though she would not have considered a relationship with him until finding common ground during their coffee date. While Dana was not against dating Todd, she might have dismissed him completely. When Todd professed his passion for old architecture and design, he was merely looking for a subtle way to connect with Dana, as he had researched and learned about her fascination with antiques. Todd didn't care about architecture, nor did he find road trips enjoyable, though he was willing to use these items of interest to convince Dana that they would be a great match, and it worked. In this situation, Todd used manipulation for the following reasons:

- He focused on his personal and professional gain from dating Dana and did not consider that she would benefit from him, nor did it concern him. Even if Dana would benefit from their relationship, this was not a factor in Todd's decision to seduce and pursue her.
- Todd stood more to gain from a potential relationship, or even working friendship, with Dana. He chose to pursue her for dating because he could find out more about her on an intimate level, giving him more advantages than his colleagues and possibly securing more business because of her influence.
- The common ground between Dana and Todd was completely fabricated, which is a form of deception because Todd had no genuine interest in her passion for antiques and road trips. By convincing Dana that they shared these hobbies in common, he led her to believe that they would make the ideal couple.

In both scenarios, persuasion, and to a degree, manipulation can be used to produce the result you want from someone, even if they are not apt to make that specific decision originally. At the very least, persuasion works on people who are heading in the same direction you want them to move, by giving them that extra push or incentive to finalize their choice, which can benefit both you and them. Manipulation is the next stage when persuasion fails, or simply isn't strong enough to get the results you want.

Developing Charisma and Charm to Influence People

The act of persuasion, manipulation, and their success depends heavily on how charismatic you are. Unless you appeal to your target or audience, you'll fail to convince anyone that you have something they want. This applies to almost every situation. Thus establishing a good rapport and sensing that the other person likes you from the start is essential. It's the foundation upon which you can build much more. Charm and charisma are natural traits for some people, who appear to put little or no effort into gaining favor with almost anyone. For most people, even those with the gift of establishing an excellent first impression, increasing the level of charisma requires keeping the other person or group in your favor for a prolonged period, until your goal is fulfilled and, or they make a decision or move in your support.

What does it take to establish and improve charisma and charm when meeting someone for the first time, and how can you achieve this without fumbling or making simple mistakes? Many factors need to be in place before you can execute your plan of action, which includes where and when you'll meet, the clothing you wear, and how well you can hold the other person's attention. It's essential to research the group or individual if you have information in advance, such as a potential client and, or candidate. If you are applying for a job or position, it's good to know as much about the company or organization you want to use, so that you can showcase your knowledge to impress the interviewer.

The following attributes are vital for developing charisma, as they set the stage for a positive script and smooth, natural flow of exchange between you and the other person or people:

- Be present and banish and preconceived ideas you may have about a specific person or what they represent when you meet them. While it is acceptable to hold an opinion or feeling about someone, any judgments you make should be placed aside. There is always a chance that what you know or learn is inaccurate, which could taint your overall impression. Approach the meeting or invitation with a fresh, clean slate and with an open mind.

- Keep your focus on the other person. If there is a group, focus on who is speaking, and nod, use eye contact periodically and if invited, contribute to the discussion or conversation. If you interrupt by mistake, quickly apologize and quickly offer the other person to continue. Give them the spotlight and validate what they say. Once they shift the discussion to you with a question or a request for detail, smile before you begin, and if you fumble, laugh at yourself and make it part of the flow. Keeping this focus will help you to break from tension, and it gives the other person a chance to see your "human" side, in addition to being a professional.

- Avoid fidgeting or playing with your phone or other devices. Most of us are so connected to our portable electronics that it can easily take our attention from a real-time conversation. People tend to view this as highly disrespectful in some circles, and some people will actively request that all devices be turned off or switched to "silent" mode. Even in the absence of instruments or tools, fidgeting with your hands or touching your face, among other nervous habits, can devalue what you say and the meaning behind it. If you feel this will be a problem, consider folding your hands on the table in front of you, leaving them there during the interview. If you use your hands to gesture during the conversation, return them to the table immediately after to ensure you avoid fidgeting. Practice at home in front of a mirror so that this becomes easy to pull off once you are ready.

- Sometimes a question or comment is vague and needs clarification. One of the most common mistakes people make is to assume they know what you need as an answer without understanding the complete question. In some interviews or meetings, you'll be asked a question like this for this very reason: it's an excellent opportunity to test your listening skills and determine if you understand what is asked of you, and, or whether you are confident enough to ask for clarification. If there is even the slightest doubt, always ask the other person to clarify. Is the question general and open to interpretation, or more specific? When an issue is accurate, providing an example that is positive and uplifting can make an excellent impression.

- Sit or stand comfortably, so that you don't feel any discomfort. Don't be afraid to shift your weight from one leg to another or change your seat or position on a chair to improve the way you feel. Any experience of discomfort can seriously mar how you behave or respond. You may reply too quickly or hastily to avoid further discussion or nod and, or agree when you intend to return to the opposite. To avoid these scenarios, always position your body comfortably on a chair, sofa, or standing to maximize your comfort during the conversation.

- Leave a space of at least 3-4 seconds before responding to a question, even if you know the exact answer that you will provide. This pause gives the interviewer or other person that you are giving the response some severe thought. They will take this as a sign that you think before you speak, which is in your favor. A person who responds too hastily or without much preparation will often make mistakes and fumble or stutter, even when they know the subject matter well. Avoid any projection of nervousness or uncertainty by taking those few seconds. The interviewer will not expect the answer immediately, like a game show, with a limited time frame to respond. Take that short period to organize your thoughts and take a deep breath before you speak.

Charisma is all about how we impress the other person with our personality and how we interact with them. If you have a sense of humor or a shared hobby with them, let that become a focus, even for just a minute. This method can effectively break the ice and give the other person a common ground with you, even if they don't know you yet. For some people, a quick compliment or close observation about someone's office décor or style is welcome, as long as it flows with the overall theme of the interview or conversation. In a more casual setting, commenting on someone's appearance may be more acceptable than a corporate meeting or business interview. Assess each parameter individually and determine which method of approach works best, without overdoing it or making it too visible that you're trying to gain someone's favor.

What should you avoid during a meeting or conversation that can impede your chances of success? There are many ways to fail by only not thinking before speaking or making a comment too quickly without regard to our audience. A positive flow can quickly turn ugly with an inappropriate joke or feedback that's taken offensively. Some blunders can derail a conversation or interaction quickly, which you should avoid as much as possible:

- When you are listening solely to respond. This practice may be well-intentioned if you want to continue a conversation and the other person enjoys talking with you. Unfortunately, this practice means you're not truly listening to what they say. You can easily miss a vital fact or comment by jumping head-first in response. When this happens, it can result in saying something irrelevant or insensitive, simply because you didn't listen well enough.

- Avoid changing the subject unless it's necessary. There are situations when changing the topic is appropriate, though usually this isn't required. The topic may be a source of passion and emotion for the other person, and skipping past it can have dire consequences. They may feel that you don't truly care about what they have to say or appreciate their input. As a result, anything you say after will have the same effect. There is a time and place to change the subject, for example: if you notice that the current subject matter is disturbing or triggering for the other person, or if the next issue is related and you know for sure that they will welcome the switch.

- Don't interrupt, because it is a sure-fire way to lose your credibility during a conversation and favor with the other person. This practice is considered rude, and it can also be a sign that you don't have the patience or timing to comment when it is appropriate to do so. Children tend to interrupt during a conversation when they feel impulsive or excited about something, though this tones down over time and is avoided as we grow into adulthood. Hold onto any important thoughts you need to share and wait until there is a break in the conversation.

- Avoid distractions, as they are primarily a concern if you are meeting on a busy street or place of business where people are always walking by and other activities are occurring. Focus on the person in front of you and see them as the anchor during the entire discussion. If you become momentarily distracted, quickly apologize and return to the conversation.

Examples of Using Charisma and Charm to Your Advantage

How can you apply the benefits of developing charisma and charm in real-life scenarios? Consider the following situations and note how each person employs various tactics to ensure they make an excellent first impression. What we learn is best put into practice as soon as possible to ensure we have a good grasp of what works best in various situations. For example, if you plan to attend a job interview, practice first with a friend or family member to get an idea of how the flow of conversation will be.

Scenario 1: The Job Interview

Samantha was excited to attend an interview for a position as assistant manager at a prestigious commercial and residential building downtown in a large urban setting. She had all the qualifications, though she knew there were many other candidates with similar credentials. Samantha wanted to make a good impression and score a strong rapport with the panel of interviewers, as this could ultimately lead to a career opportunity in property management. To prepare for the interview, Samantha researched the management company currently under contract with the building, as well as the history of the area, the demographics, and other characteristics that could prove useful. She wore professional attire and brought a printed copy of her resume, cover letter, and references to the interview. Samantha was nervous but also confident that she possessed the right skill set for the job.

The panel interviewed a boardroom with glass walls, allowing a view to the outside. The company was busy, with a regular flow of people coming and going. Samantha was excited about the modern décor and prestige associated with the company that she nearly forgot where the office was located, which almost made her late. Fortunately, she asked someone in the corridor and quickly made her way into the boardroom before the interview began. Upon arriving, the full panel of interviewers was there, ready to engage in small talk and conversation before the official meeting. Samantha took advantage of this opportunity to talk about her favorite sports team and her love of cycling outdoors. When the interview began, Samantha made sure she was prepared to answer questions like "Why do you want to work for us?" and "What makes a good property manager?" The interviewers sensed that Samantha was eager to please others and may encounter challenges when saying no to a client at a job site. They presented a few scenarios that featured difficult-to-manage people and best practices in responding to them.

Samantha listened carefully to each scenario, pausing before she responded. They were a bit more challenging to answer than expected, but she did her best to find the right way to reply. In the second scenario, Samantha provided two solution options that she hoped would be correct. Towards the end of the interview, the panel asked Samantha if she had any questions. Despite being well prepared for the interview, she hadn't anticipated being asked this and was afraid to say that she hadn't any inquiries, so she asked about the company's history and development plans. This seemed to resonate with the group, and she felt good about the interview in general. Samantha was told that she would receive a call to attend a follow-up second interview if she was considered a suitable candidate.

Assessment of Scenario 1

Samantha did a great job of preparing for the interview and struck a good rapport with the panel. They enjoyed the conversation with her and noticed that she had a high degree of knowledge about the firm and was eager to learn more. Samantha wasn't the most experienced in property management but did provide a lot of additional, transferable skills that she included in her interview, which gave everyone a favorable impression. When considering Samantha's overall presentation, how well did she perform? Following the discussion, the panel of interviewers discussed Samantha's meeting and thought about whether she would be a good fit. They enjoyed how quickly she responded when asked a few industry-related questions with specific scenarios. In reviewing their next group of candidates, they decided to give Samantha another chance. She seemed polite and agreeable, which was good for building rapport with colleagues and clients; however, she would need a stronger resolve to handle difficult situations on the job. The second interview would allow her to display more of her problem-solving skills and determine if she would be a good fit.

Scenario 2: The Development Proposal

Darren was interested in presenting an idea to his town council. As part of a developing company, he had his eyes set on building a new complex that would provide a space for stores and apartments or condominiums above. He had an ambitious idea that would not resonate well with everyone. A similar proposal was presented a few years ago with an overwhelmingly negative reaction. Many of the town's residents wanted to preserve the historical value of the buildings and didn't take well to modern developments, even if the original structures remained the same and untouched.

Before his scheduled meeting with Darren, the town council had always been divided on further proposals. They were keen on keeping their town in its original state, despite the chances, there could be more tourism and opportunities for revenue. Darren came prepared. He knew the objection he faced and was ready to deal with it. Having lived in the town for three years, he had a wife and kids who were actively involved in the community. They were well-liked and respected. Darren would use this information to his advantage and highlight the need for the town council to look into the future.

Upon meeting the council one evening, Darren approached the table eagerly, but not too much, so that he wouldn't appear too much like a salesperson. The reception was friendly and cordial. Half of the council was already in favor of the development, so Darren knew he had to convince a few more people to give it a chance. He appealed to the fact that most council members had families and enjoyed the local businesses in town. Since the economic downturn, the town's business suffered, forcing at least two shops to close and more to downsize. Upon presenting these facts and evoking an emotional response from most people, he finally offered his plan of development as a new way to resolve the town's problems.

Almost immediately after unveiling the plan and proposing the structure, Darren met with opposition from two members. He wanted to interrupt, as they had responded with incorrect information about the project, but he restrained himself and let them voice their concerns. Once they finished, Darren explained his awareness of a previous plan and how it wasn't received well. He expressed that his idea was unlike the previous proposal, which was much larger and would negatively impact the view of the city and impact small businesses.

Darren explained that if the town council was willing to listen to his version or upgrade the idea, that he would happily provide them with more information to give them more details on his vision. The council agreed to listen to Darren, and they were surprised to learn that the scale of the project was much smaller than previously imagined. There would also be communal spaces inside the building for local artisans and business owners to showcase and promote their brands.

Upon reviewing the full plans, the council ushered a collective sigh of relief, yet they were left with some indecision. The council decided that giving the new proposal a review, which was more in favor of the majority of residents, would be fair to reconsider, as the town did encounter an economic downturn, and they needed good ideas to bring more tourism. The proposal didn't guarantee an increased flow of business, nor did it plan to improve tourists; however, the potential for becoming a good source of revenue for residents and improving their morale was a good reason to reconsider.

Assessment of Scenario 2

Darren was well prepared and brought a lot of information to the table during the town council's meeting. He was able to take a back seat to listen to everyone's concerns while offering a concerned, thoughtful approach to the town's problems while introducing a new proposal that was not the same as before. He was ready to wait and understood the plight of the town council. Darren highlighted the fact that while he was a new resident, his family was happy, involved in the community, and they were there to stay. While Darren was eager to respond to pushback from the members of the council, he kept his thoughts until everyone was ready and willing to listen. This worked effectively in his favor because had he responded too quickly, they would feel pushed or manipulated. Darren's persuasion worked because he appealed to the fears and concerns of the individuals, as well as the residents of the town. He presented realistic ideas and solutions that he had already incorporated into his plans.

After the council meeting, the members gave the idea more thought and consideration. Collectively, the council was divided, though they did see a place for the new proposal in their future. They also noted how it was important to consider new ideas for reviving their town while preserving the history of their residents. The proposal didn't immediately lead to a full agreement, though it did shift the conversation to a more agreeable stance: to reconsider some form of development, whether or not it was fully in line with Darren's plan or not, and to invite more proposals to give the town more options to choose from. While the council meeting wasn't a full win-win for Darren, it gave him a shot at bidding on a final project option, which would be reviewed for a final decision at a later date.

CHAPTER 4
Neuro-Linguistic Programming (Nlp)

What Is NLP or Neuro-Linguistic Programming?

Neuro-linguistic programming is a method that applies aspects of psychology and analysis to assess other people, their language, and actions to communicate and achieve specific outcomes. This practice focuses on recognizing patterns and using strategies that produce a specific experience or situation that can be mutually beneficial or provide an advantage to one person or party. NLP is a widely accepted practice in many fields of work and by individuals who want to improve and enhance their understanding and connection with other people. It is a powerful way to gain a healthy level of influence over another person or group. People who are skilled in using NLP can captivate a broad audience for hours. This level of expertise is possible, and it can be applied in practice by anyone willing to learn the various techniques of this practice and apply them consistently.

The History, Development, and Effectiveness of NLP: A History of its Development and Implementation in Various Aspects of Business and Personal Life

In the 1970s, NLP (neuro-linguistic programming) was developed by John Grinder and Richard Bandler, by observing and documenting specific patterns in communication, both verbal and non-verbal, and how they could be used to understand cognitive functions better. During this decade, further research and studies indicated a connection between how patterns in the way we talk or gesture could provide an in-depth glimpse into the mind, and how we interact with others using subtle, yet effective communication can influence and, or bring about specific results. As NLP was further developed and understood, it became used as a tool for many professions, including business, counseling, law, sports, education, and many other fields.

Understanding and applying NLP focuses on the underlying map or programming within our mind that each of us possesses, which gives us a "personal map" or blueprint of our experience in life. NLP builds on this concept by using senses and communication techniques to process and learn from other people while influencing them and understanding them better. Each personal map is formed and developed by how we perceive and interact with the outside world. The information we receive through our senses and how we experience it is unique to ourselves, and this varies from one individual to another. To better understand another person and how they think and behave, NLP attempts to match or mirror the individual's behavior to gain access to the inner "personal map," which provides feedback in the form of gestures, posture and stances, and other cues, both verbal and non-verbal.

NLP is useful in many ways. It is a powerful tool for influencing people and convincing them to behave and act in specific ways, which can play a dominant, influential role in dark psychology and how using these techniques can result in getting what you want. Imagine having the ability to understand how someone else's mind and behavior work, so that you can effectively use these patterns in your favor to gain from it. In the professional realm, NLP is applied in therapy to gauge and get "inside the mind" of patients by following their unique patterns and prescribing a better treatment plan. Business, marketing, and sales fields were heavily influenced by NLP tactics, which observe the potential client or customer by their actions. For example, a person readily available to make a purchase or invest in a product or service may display certain gestures or cues as a sign of "openness" in their body language or tone. Hand and eye movements are recognized as a powerful means to determine if someone is lying or avoiding a particular topic or situation. This practice can be a resourceful point in understanding people both professionally and personally.

What Are the Benefits of NLP?

Aside from developing useful tools with NLP that can enhance your ability to influence and gain the advantage in one-on-one and group situations, how can this practice benefit you personally?

- You will develop new and better strategies for solving problems. Learning and practicing NLP is the result of knowing how to think like other people and looking beyond how your mind works by examining others. The more practice you gain by employing NLP skills, you will soon have a new set of tools for future issues.
- With regular practice, and by nature, you'll abandon useless and repetitive ways of thinking and acting that have led you

nowhere in the past. NLP aligns your mind and thinking with new, innovative ways to understand yourself as well as other people. Through discovering new ideas and techniques and having the ability to influence and connect with people on a different level, you'll have a better sense of how your actions and behavior impact others. For example, you will be more effective in coaching and training people, and your words and gestures will have more meaning and impact.

- A sale is a challenging field, and most people understand that the level of negotiation and influence on others is vital for closing. NLP gives you the ability to negotiate effectively by knowing your "target" or the other person by their body language and subtle cues. You will benefit tremendously from NLP techniques and improve the trajectory of your career, especially if your line of business is sales or marketing.
- NLP has the effect of creating a more balanced effect on your body and mind. The primary objective of NLP is to anchor your state of mind and to be in the current or present. With measured breathing and analyzing your thoughts, you'll become aware of which habits or thinking patterns are best to overcome or change for better mental health and overall wellbeing. Reducing stress is one of the most important aspects of life today, and in doing so, you'll have a better grasp on your life and goals ahead. On the other hand, practicing NLP can harness more energy in your life and give you a stronger sense of purpose and vitality that you may not have experienced before.
- More power and greater control over your life and the effect(s) of other people's control over you will change significantly. You will gain a better level of influence over other people. You will also achieve greater success by taking more power over your own life. This practice will lead to more and consistent progress over time.
- Confidence will increase, and this will position you to achieve in life. People tend to listen more intently when you demonstrate self-esteem and believe in yourself.
- Improving your ability to speak publicly and address a group will improve as you increase your confidence and knowledge through NLP.

- NLP not only gives you insight into other people's thought processes and emotions but yours as well. By learning how to read your own body's signals, you will recognize when something is "off" or does not feel normal. This can give you a sense of when you need to make changes to your lifestyle (diet, eating, exercise, etc.) or when you "listen" to your body and make proactive decisions to improve the quality of life.
- NLP can give you the power to face and conquer negative patterns and habits such as addiction and other compulsive behaviors that cause more harm than benefit.
- Achieving leadership is closer than you think, and this can be accomplished with NLP, by leveraging what you learn, know, and practice with other people to gain their confidence in you. This can ultimately give you the advantage in situations where you may be a candidate for a promotion or higher position within your company.

Whether you intend to apply NLP techniques for work or personal purposes, you will find that learning this system can boldly improve your chances of success. Understanding and developing skills associated with this practice can lead you to influence other people's thoughts and reactions, but it can also improve behavior and shape the way other people perceive you. This method will give you a better connection to other people's thoughts and emotions, which can give you a significant advantage in many situations.

CHAPTER 5
Developing Nlp Skills

How to Decipher Other People's True Feelings, Thoughts, and Emotions Through NLP Techniques

As amazing and unbelievable as it sounds, NLP (neuro-linguistic programming) provides many techniques that can sharpen your ability to understand and "decode" the most difficult people to read. Many people that we encounter or meet send us signals or cues that hint at their true intentions, even if what they say is the opposite. While there are numerous tactics you can choose from, there are a set of standard practices that you can learn in preparation for your next meeting.

Anchoring

This technique works by creating an association or a connection between an emotion and an action. Anchoring is a technique applied in therapy and life coaching situations where the client is asked to think of a passion or feeling that is perceived as positive. For example, they may think of happiness or a sense of excitement; then, they must choose an action to link or associate with the emotion, such as tapping their elbow and snapping their fingers. When this connection is established, it allows the person to experience the full extent of the emotion by using the action to bring it about. When their fingers snap, or they touch their elbow, the sensation of the feeling will surface, which gives them the full experience at that moment. This technique creates new memories centering around positive emotions by invoking them into effect with an action. This practice can help people manage their feelings and help them come to terms with certain thoughts and feelings by giving them greater control.

This same technique is applied to control the way other people perceive a situation or thought. For example, if the same or similar action is initiated by someone else, this may produce a related, positive feeling in the person who is "programmed" with this anchoring technique. A person could easily use this tactic to invoke a sensation of contentment in a group or crowd of people, by using anchoring to link an action or spoken word with positive emotion.

Mirroring and Building Rapport

Mirroring is a technique used to build and develop a rapport with someone. It is a subtle yet effective way of observing the mannerisms and gestures of another person and gently mirroring or copying these movements so that they are not too noticeable. Subconsciously, this mirroring technique draws the other person closer to you, as it is natural to relate to someone else who uses the same body language. In effect, you are communicating with them through body language, and as you mirror their actions, they will synchronize and copy in return. Mirroring and building rapport establish a connection with them and allows them to build an environment with you where they feel comfortable and trusting. This option opens the door to expressing more emotion and feeling, in effect, allowing the other person to let their guard down. Consider this example: the mirroring technique could result in changing the behavior of a client from agitated to more relaxed, by gently mirroring their body language, then adjusting your movements to encourage a more comfortable stance or position. You might smile or nod, which in turn, prompts similar behavior from the other person, who feels more inclined to follow the positive lead and express themselves more readily.

Visualization through the use of Hypnosis and Meditation

Hypnosis and meditation can help you guide or lead other people to visualize success or other pleasant thoughts associated with a specific goal or thinking pattern. This method is an effective way to help people abandon their negative thinking habits and focus on visuals that stimulate positive reflection and association with certain activities or ideas. To convince someone that they must associate an idea or thought you have, such as a pleasant view of a beachfront property or scenic cabin in the woods, you can "draw" these images in your client's mind through the power of hypnosis and suggestion. This practice will guide them into a meditative state. Once this association or link between the goal and visualization is established, the other person will be able to associate the thought with a pleasant image. This will create an incentive to move further in this direction. The ability to use suggestion and imagery is an impactful way to influence others and give them a visual "guide" or incentive to strengthen your impact on them.

Reframing Your Thoughts

This technique involves taking a negative thought and altering it to fit into a positive mindset. For example, consider an individual who struggles with several medical conditions directly related to the way they eat. They know that if they make changes to their meal plan, there is a good chance of improvement. The internal thought process or pattern may revolve around statements such as "I don't want to be sick" or "I don't want to get worse." While these seem positive, they contain the word "don't," which is a negative. The brain registers these statements with the emphasis on words like "sick" and "worse," which changes the context significantly. The word "don't" doesn't factor into the mind's interpretation of each sentence, which means it must be positive to be effective. This thought process can subconsciously prevent many people from improving their health, and they can be defeating their success as a result. The NLP technique of framing or reframing your thinking process involves changing the following statements to include a more proactive approach:

- From "I don't want to be sick" to "I want to get well." The focus is shifted from "sick" to "well," which is a more positive angle.

- From "I don't want to get worse" to "I want to get better." The focus is shifted from "worse" to "better," which takes the negative wording and transfers the statement into a more positive tone.

In the above examples, the focus is shifted away from what the person doesn't want or wants to refrain from, and instead redirected towards the goal of improving your health and feeling better. This has a powerful impact on the level of success and focus. It can be narrowed down to include a more specific approach, such as "I want to improve my diet" as more than a result, but also a method, by changing the way you eat. "I want to get fit and feel good" refers to aiming towards exercise and making the most out of its benefits.

A Change in Belief or Perspective

We often find that our perspective of ourselves distorts from how others see us. We also hold beliefs or opinions that are important to us, though some ideas about ourselves are negative and serve no purpose in self-development and progress. A common and problematic mindset occurs when a belief contributes to self-sabotage. It becomes a repeated statement or mantra in our mind that we struggle with. Examples of such statements include "I can't succeed at school" or "I'm not capable of success," or more specific statements that devalue our abilities. Unfortunately, many people hear these statements in childhood or at a young age, and they simply stick in our minds without good reason. NLP can change this direction by changing the way we think and perceive ourselves and our situations. This outcome occurs by focusing on our current state of mind, then directing where we want to go, and influencing the mind in a way that can bring about a change in perception and focus. NLP is based on a list of principles or suppositions that link closely the mind and body together, along with behavior and communication. When our body, mind, thoughts, and perceptions align along with behavior, collectively, this can alter the path we take with the power of suggestion and the tools or skills within us. Giving people a sense of empowerment is an opportunistic way to instill thoughts and ideas at the same time, by improving their state of mind, they will be more open and accepting of change and input, even if it is not completely aligned with their own.

Study in Body Language and Non-Verbal Communication

NLP is a robust system that can work wonders for how you communicate with other people and influence them. It is essential to understand and observe body language and non-verbal cues to master the tactics of manipulation and persuasion. These activities are just as important, and in some cases, more vital to understanding what a person means or wants to say than what they say. Reading body language is essential to know how and when to respond. Listening skills are imperative to establishing a connection with someone, though reading beyond what they say verbally is the heart of human nature and signals more about what we want. Consider the following example:

A man asks a woman passing by for directions to a specific store. She stops to assist him, and while she smiles and behaves cordially, she folds her arms across her chest and keeps a significant distance. Once the information exchanges, they move in their respective and intended directions after pleasantly ending the conversation. The perception of the woman could be viewed as friendly and comfortable because she was willing to stop and help with directions. Alternatively, noticing the tightly guarded stance and folded arms could signal someone who is not keen on being friendly, but chose to do so because it is a socially acceptable practice. The woman may have looked guarded without intending to do so, but rather as a reaction to simply not knowing the man. If he was a neighbor or friend, her posture and disposition could be more relaxed.

Understanding the nature of body language means reading cues and aligning them with what the person is saying. If someone states they like the taste of their meal but scrunch their face in reaction, you wouldn't believe them. Similarly, a person who pretends they are happy for you, only to grimace their face in discontent, can indicate a hidden layer or envy or jealousy. There are key areas to focus your attention on when reading people and determining what they mean to say and why.

Eye Movements

The way someone looks at you, whether they avert your glance or stare at you intensely, say a lot about their intention. When a person blinks rapidly, or their pupils dilate, they may be nervous or stressed. This motion could mean they have a lot going on internally, though choose not to disclose much during a conversation. If a person fixates on someone or something, it could be a sign that they want to be recognized or noticed. If they look at a specific object, they may wish to use or examine it closer. Alternatively, glancing away can signal avoidance from a particular person or object.

Proximity and Posture

When someone stands close to you, they usually feel comfortable and at ease. They may be testing you to see if you move away or accept the closeness, which means they can react accordingly. When someone keeps their distance, this occurs for several reasons: there is a lack of comfort to move closer. For some people, keeping their distance is normal, and how they prefer to approach a stranger or someone they are not familiar with on an intimate level. It's not always personal, but culture, where keeping a certain distance, is not only familiar by expected as a sign of respect and acknowledging your own space.

Head Movements

When someone nods their head, this is usually a sign of agreement or acknowledgment. A slow nod can indicate a strong agreement while nodding vigorously can mean that the person is keen on finishing the conversation and, or needs to go. Tilting the head to one side can signal that someone is listening and observing intently while moving the head backward can be a sign of suspicion or doubt about what someone is saying or doing. Always pay attention to how people look at each other in a group, and how often they repeat these head movements. When a person is constantly or regularly staring at someone specifically, they may be looking for a reaction or approval in the form of a smile or nod. On the other hand, avoiding someone or observing everyone in the room, but them is a sign that the person doesn't regard them as essential or worthy of attention. They may also feel intimidated and want to avoid looking at someone who has a strong effect on them.

Hand Signals and Arm Movements

One of the most expressive ways to communicate non-verbally is by using your hands, whether you dismiss someone with a casual wave or point at them in an accusatory manner. Fingers and hands account for a great deal of how we express what we feel with other people. When someone is bored or tired, they usually prop their head with their hand and lean against the table with their elbow propping them. Shaky hands can indicate nervousness or fear, a fist can signal frustration or anger, even if the person has no intention of acting violently or expressing their feelings. Hiding hands in pockets or behind the back can hint that there's something deceit or sneakiness. There are many other hand signals and gestures that indicate many other cues about people and their true intentions. Arm movements are often an extension of the hands, and usually exaggerate or embellish gestures. When someone uses their arms in a large, circular motion, or by holding them out as if to invite an embrace, which is also a sign of friendliness and feeling welcome. This action can also indicate that they want your attention. Alternatively, folding the arms across the chest is a sign of avoidance or nervousness. This can also indicate a lack of trust or feeling unsafe in a specific situation. Placing the hands on your hips is a sign of exerting dominance or feeling impatient.

Mouth and Facial Gestures

In addition to how eyes shift and give away someone's innermost thoughts, the way we smile or twist our facial expression also speaks more than the words we say. If someone presents a broad smile, this can be a good sign of happiness or a sign of approval. A smirk or half-smile can indicate mischievousness or sarcasm. When a smile appears too good or exaggerated, it may be fake or a sign that the person is trying too hard to impress or convince you they are happy, even when this is false. Pursed lips are usually an indication that someone is upset or disappointed, whereas a relaxed face shows positivity and a calm disposition. Many people will use their faces to hide their true feelings, though often, their eyes may convey a different emotion or sign from their mouth.

Once you begin to observe and notice various facial expressions and body gestures, it becomes easier to understand what people think and feel outside of their verbal expressions. There are many other ways in which a person can reveal their true intention and feelings when they interact with you, whether they notice it themselves or not. When you make the distinction between what people want to convey and their true expression, you discover that it is a vital way to read and understand people and connect with them and use this knowledge to your advantage.

Using Neuro-Linguistic Programming to Your Advantage with Non-Verbal Gestures, Cues, and Language

As you learn and become accustomed to both deciphering and using various forms of communication with other people, you'll notice some significant advantages. This practice is due to knowing your audience and choosing to learn more from observation. By looking beyond the surface, you'll discover that many people, as predictable as we can be, hide and manipulate without realizing they are doing so. Consider the simple example of someone asking how you are. Most people respond to "how are you?" with "I'm fine," which is usually the only (or mostly) satisfactory reply to this question. Any truthful response that explains how bad your week is going to hints at another form of displeasure is often hidden. People inherently know that the only answer most of us use is "I'm fine" or "I'm ok" and will often respond in this way, though their body language and general behavior will give away their true feelings.

How can using NLP become a benefit in everyday situations and regularly? By using these techniques, you will develop a better understanding of how the mind works, and how we can harness that ability to connect with people using these thought and mind patterns to our advantage. Learning about other people is not only possible with NLP skills, but this practice can also be applied in a way that gives other people a sense that you understand them thoroughly. NLP offers opportunities when we understand how to communicate and mirror other people effectively in a wide range of situations and conversations:

- The other person will open and give you more information about themselves once they feel comfortable with you. Mirroring and gesturing in a subtle but similar manner to the other person will provide them with a sense of familiarity, and they are more likely to connect with you.
- When communicating with someone based on their non-verbal cues and gestures that speak louder and more specific and genuine than their words, you give them the idea that you understand them on a much deeper level.
- Observing other people helps us re-evaluate ourselves too. We may realize that the way someone gestures and gives away their true intentions could be a trait that we use as well. By understanding why some people use specific methods over others, we can determine which gestures and body language we use and how they affect the way other people communicate with us.

NLP is ideal for understanding human nature and how we interact with ourselves, each other, and the environment. Taking the time to learn and apply NLP practices and techniques can provide a great way to understand and apply concepts about how we relate to one another. When you understand how to over serve and notice the importance of non-verbal cues and gestures in everyday life, you'll always have the advantage.

CHAPTER 6
Examples Of Scenarios In Applying Dark Psychology Techniques

Examples and Scenarios on the Power of Influence and Applying Dark Psychology Techniques

How can you use dark psychology techniques to gain favor and advance in your career, community, and life? Once you have the essential tools and ideas and learn how to apply them, a few examples of how dark psychology works and the different levels you can use will give you a more in-depth look at how real scenarios are manipulated. Whether you use gentle or moderate forms of persuasion or apply stronger, manipulative techniques, there are ways to get what you want. The following scenarios are examples of how specific situations can benefit an individual when certain tactics are applied.

Scenario 1: The New Mechanic

Jason recently moved into a town to start a new job as a mechanic. He was eager to meet people and secure some friendships and quickly learned that many of the town's residents were polite, though slow to respond with the same enthusiasm. After two months, Jason began to feel that he would not fit into the community, despite his success at work. He decided to read about psychology and how he could appeal more to other people. He wanted to gain social acceptance, and eventually open his own mechanic business, though he needed both the support and rapport with residents to make it work.

A close friend visited Jason, and they talked at length about his dilemma. His friend, Lily, suggested he study NLP as a way to unlock the mystery of people in the small town and fully understand how to appeal to them. Not only will he be able to connect on their level as a friend and neighbor, but Lily also explained that NLP could give him the ability to "tap" into the way other people think and behave in such a way that he can effectively influence them in his favor. This idea was an exciting prospect for Jason, and he proceeded to study this practice for his benefit.

NLP techniques provided an exciting glimpse into the way others behave and why. Jason soon discovered that many people felt intimidated or unsure of him because of his overly friendly nature, and having no previous ties to the town. Some people who avoided eye contact or stood with strained posture were less open to suggestion and connection, while other people in town were slowly receptive to Jason. He quickly learned how understanding and following specific patterns would create a distinct advantage, and it did: within several weeks, Jason attended a barbeque and house party. These events allowed him further access to meeting more people and getting to know those he knew already. By simply engaging with people differently, Jason began to notice significant changes in the way others took notice of him and were more likely to let their guard down.

Building a network gave Jason a good foundation for starting a business. Despite his employer, a well-established mechanic, Jason would introduce competition into the town, and his relationship with prominent people in the local area could lead to future investors, stakeholders, and customers. He would need to develop a more robust, more persuasive technique to convince people to visit his shop, and effectively, remove long-time customers of his former employer. Jason considered his options for promoting his new business: he could circulate flyers or buy ads to offer a discount rate and undercut his competition. While this proposal was certain to cause division in the town, Jason was keen on stroking the egos of those with leadership and attending the town's social functions regularly. This gave him more favor, and more people entrusted him over time, which would eventually work to his advantage. Further engagement increased his customer base, which was an added benefit to securing strong relationships within the community.

Jason's persuasive techniques proved successful, though he encountered pushback from many of the town's residents. Some individuals considered him to be manipulative and guilty of destroying his former employer's reputation. When confronted about this, Jason would use his charisma and carefully crafted wording to explain healthy competition, and he never meant any harm to the other mechanic, despite taking away some of his business. Jason was successful for many years, and the other mechanic soon retired early, which residents blamed on his slowing market. Some residents continued to enjoy the new mechanic in town, while others were disappointed by the changes and often considered Jason to be an imposter.

Assessment of Scenario 1

In reviewing Jason's scenario, how persuasive and, or manipulative did he have to become to convince people to leave their regular mechanic and conduct business with him instead, despite having just recently moved into town without any connections? When Jason accepted the position with the small town's mechanic, he used this opportunity to survey the town and to get to know the residents. He noticed they enjoyed a simple and predictable lifestyle, and they weren't too keen on welcoming a stranger with no ties to their community. A few attempts at conversation didn't get Jason far, and his goal was to secure a positive reputation in town and to build his mechanic shop. This would eventually place him in a position to take on the role of his employer. This proposal would require more than friendly chatting and waving hello to neighbors. Jason needed to gain the upper hand and secure his place in the community before he could advance any further.

When Lily introduced Jason to NLP, he quickly took action to learn and apply the techniques. Jason was not afraid to gain the upper hand and use any form of manipulation possible. However, he preferred to gradually work his way into the hearts of the town and not appear too ambitious or greedy. Jason researched the town's history, and more specifically, if they had any other mechanics or similar competition over the past ten years. He quickly discovered that not only did his employer hold a monopoly over the town, but he also charged more than average. He didn't involve himself socially in the town's events. This gave Jason a clear advantage: he could run for the town council and get involved by "giving back" and volunteering for the community. Once his business was ready to open, he could undercut the competition and offer the residents a better deal.

Getting involved with the community gave Jason the advantage of building a rapport with the town, and it won him more favor and a positive image as well. He also managed to get elected to the town council; after demonstrating his commitment to the town's needs and getting involved in fundraising, Jason won over more people than expected. He pitched his shop ideas to a few prominent members of the town, and they appeared in favor of his direction.

When Jason first opened the doors to his new shop, he was greeted with mixed reviews, though over a year, more people became customers. Some people still considered him an imposter or an unwelcome resident, while others were grateful for the healthy competition.

Jason's techniques could be seen as manipulative because he hid his real agenda from everyone until he was ready to take action. He only confided in a few people, including the town's more affluent population, as he became familiar with them when running for the town council. He carefully orchestrated all of his moves to align with the grand prize: a successful, profitable business in a picturesque town that he could call home. Jason was not only good at gaining favor with most of the small town, and he did so within the short span of one year before opening his shop.

Scenario 2: Controlling the Store Staff

Hanna was a supervisor for a retail store. When she accepted the promotion, it was a welcome change, though the staff was notoriously tricky to manage. She noticed they would try to sneak out early and expect to be paid for the full hours, while some would arrive late frequently. The manager of the store was fully aware of these behaviors and was ready to hand out written warnings to the offenders when Hanna asked if she could try to work with the employees to curb their habits. The manager gave her two weeks to give it a shot. The next day, Hanna scheduled a meeting with all the staff. As expected, not everyone showed, and half of them arrived late. Hanna made a formal introduction of herself as the new supervisor and set down some rules that she expected everyone to follow, including:

- No more late arrivals unless it is an emergency. Always call before arriving late.
- Breaks need to be taken at their predetermined time, according to the schedule, and not before or after.
- Leaving too soon is not acceptable, and result in pay deductions for the time missed.

Among these rules, there were further items discussed, and while the staff generally agreed to follow them, Hanna noticed the opposite was right after the first week. She sent a reminder email to everyone about the meeting, only to be disregarded and ignored. Hanna knew this matter would only worsen, and while some of the employees would likely receive a warning or dismissal, she had other plans to handle the situation. Throughout a weekend, Hanna made a point of learning everyone's habits and schedules. She noticed that the weekly schedule posted with the employees' preferences was noted and that the previous supervisor gave in to the staff, often overworking. Hanna knew they wouldn't listen to her directly, so she came up with a new plan of updating the schedule weekly, but only if each employee submitted their request by a strict deadline. The way Hanna communicated to the staff ensured they would receive and know this information in advance, and each record of correspondence was kept on file, in case anyone challenged her methods. Furthermore, anyone late or absent without proper notice would forfeit their ability to request certain days off.

Once the employees realized the seriousness of these changes, they had varying reactions. Some felt that Hanna was manipulative because she didn't give them notice of her intentions to restrict their schedules, and yet, she never scolded or caused any reason for anyone to file a complaint. Hanna decided to meet with each of the employees on a one-on-one basis to review their position and performance. Some of the staff found this to be intimidating, though she was ready to act. Hanna recently read about NLP and how to use the skills of persuasion and mirroring other people's actions to learn their intentions and react accordingly. She expected a lot of resistance, though most of the staff were willing to engage, and divulged a lot about themselves either verbally or with specific cues. When Hanna listened to them and observed their actions and behaviors, she was able to connect well with each employee. This technique helped her influence their work habits positively. As a result, the employees felt more attached to their jobs and recognized better than other supervisors in the past. The staff's loyalty grew, which also improved their performance and morale. Some of the employees avoided being late or leaving early out of fear of losing their job.

Assessment of Scenario 2

Did Hanna use persuasion or manipulation to enforce her strict rules as a supervisor? Initially, she threatened disciplinary action if employees didn't comply with the regulations. They found this to be severe because no one had enforced these rules before, and as a result, Hanna was expected to re-establish the guidelines. Hanna decided to take a more persuasive or direct approach towards the staff, though she met with no response nor changes initially, which meant more robust steps had to be taken. The employees initially found Hanna harsh, however once met with them individually, this allowed her to connect more one-on-one, securing a better relationship, but one with a set of conditions. She simultaneously instilled a sense of fear (of losing employment) while establishing a good rapport and understanding with the staff overall. Manipulation was applied to gain more control over the store and employees, which not only improved their performance but resulted in winning over the approval of management.

CHAPTER 7
How To Further Develop And Advance Your Skills To The Next Level

Recognizing Manipulative Tactics in Others, So That You Can Gain Better Control of Situations and Conversations

When we sharpen our skills of persuasion and focus on the ideal outcome of a situation, it's important to recognize the same attributes in other people. Not everyone will easily slip into a state of influence and control. While some people may be receptive in some situations, this isn't always consistent, and timing can play an important role. As you observe other people and their behaviors, you may be under the microscope as well. For this reason, it is essential to recognize manipulative tactics in other people, so that you can know how they use them, how to learn from these techniques, and gain the advantage.

When you first meet someone, do they compliment you consistently and make you feel special and loved? This technique is a common practice used in high control groups (also known as cults), pyramid sales, and other schemes that aim to make people feel included and accepted. This tactic is successful at reeling people in to join a group and comply with rules to gain and maintain acceptance. Some people are more likely to join and become vulnerable to influence by a group or charismatic leader than others. You may find that these people are well versed in the tactics of manipulation, and in particular, love-bombing, which is the tactic used to lure people in by making them think they are truly accepted. This is a powerful practice that is usually targeted towards marginalized individuals or people who feel they are outcasts from society. Knowing the signs of love-bombing means, you can avoid the headache of finding the intention of the person or group they belong to. Once they convince someone to join a group or attend a series of meetings or events, the love-bombing or unconditional acceptance is stripped away to reveal true intentions. They may later "guilt" their target into staying with them or their group to produce high volume sales or recruit members to continue receiving favor or become outcast.

Charisma and charm will get you somewhere, especially if you are an excellent conversationalist and know how to talk to anyone. Be wary that you may simultaneously become the target of someone trying to use this technique on you in unsuspecting situations. If you appear alone or vulnerable, even if this is not the case, you may be approached by someone who feels they can target you in a way that will benefit them. If you're familiar with this practice, you'll likely recognize it right away. This tactic usually starts with a compliment or comment that grabs your attention. There are various reasons it's applied: to gain your attraction for dating or sex or to get to know you more for business or sales. If you feel that someone is genuine, take it slowly and watch for signs of impulsion. They may be skilled at remembering your name or try to use the information you provide to them to understand you more. Always keep your answers vague and advance with further details only when you feel that it is safe to do so.

The advantage of charisma as a skill can mean the difference between continuously failed connections and a strong network of business and personal relationships. It also involves two sides, where using your beauty and attraction can advance your interests, though you may also find yourself in the hands of someone using the same techniques against you. Never underestimate the power of charm and how it can play you, even if it's a tool that you apply as well. It's an easy, sleight-of-hand way to influence and direct someone's attention and favor towards you by merely striking a friendly conversation and making them feel good, and developing charisma and charm as a skillset is vital to improving your chances of making a good impression at work and in social circles. At the very least, you can build more reliable and longer-lasting rapport with more people over time.

Common Mistakes to Avoid and Improving Upon Your Skills

When you learn the principles of dark psychology techniques, including NLP, hypnosis, and other tactics involving persuasion and manipulation, you'll want to avoid pitfalls that are a barrier to success. Many mistakes are preventable when you pay close attention to your surroundings and people or the target audience.

1. Never assume you know someone better than you do. People can use deception in the same way as any of us, and in some cases, they are experts at it. While some attributes

are apparent in the cues and behaviors that we notice at first, there is often more details and information about an individual that we will need time to understand and plan our methods.

2. If you are new to practicing NLP or aspire to read or understand people better, take your time to understand all the cues and patterns. This practice will help you avoid making misjudgments, and unless you are already well versed in reading people, take the time to understand as much as possible first, before executing your program of action. Making a premature move can result in foiling any plan you have and ruin any changes you have in reattempting in the future.

3. Focus on what you know and your strengths. Jumping into unfamiliar territory or with people with whom you can't read well can lead to disaster. Make a point to research your target first, especially if you are attending an event meeting new people for the first time. This will give you a good indication of what subjects or approach will impress them and grab their attention, and help you avoid making comments or a pitch that will be lost or brushed aside.

4. Don't give away too much of your intentions, until the timing is right. When you plan to open a business or make a pitch, for example, your audience may assume you have an ulterior motive and avoid you initially. Instead, make a connection first, and drop the pitch until you have their undivided attention and respect. This technique will better secure a chance at success once you deliver your proposal.

5. Approach your target in a manner that is like their own personality or mannerisms. This option will make a better connection with them, even if just by observing how they talk and act. Behaving too aggressive or eager, especially in the beginning, can dismantle any attempt you have at securing a chance to succeed. Subtle moves and actions are often more effective because they don't appear evident and avoidable.

6. Assess the full situation before you act. This includes the person or people, their circumstance and demeanor, and overall setting. A person can behave vastly differently in one place or situation than another, which is an important factor to consider, as they may not respond the same all the time.

When an individual becomes enthusiastic about attending a specific event, such as a concert, a different approach should be used than if you were to meet with them in a more subdued atmosphere, which requires a change in tactics. By changing your disposition, you're adapting to the mood and occasion, which also makes the interaction with the person more influential.

Focusing on the Benefit of Knowing the Weaknesses of Others and Your Own

How can dark psychology provide a benefit to you? In what ways do our weaknesses and those of others have an impact on the outcome of a situation? When we use persuasive techniques, we make observations to figure out which tactics work best for a specific scenario. As we sharpen our skills in this regard, we also learn valuable aspects about ourselves that we may not have considered before. This method includes uncovering hidden fears and weaknesses that we may notice in others, but not ourselves. This realization will help us understand other people and sheds some light on how we are perceived too.

How do you react when you receive criticism? Are you immediately offended and defend yourself, internalize it and respond later, or simply brush it off? Not everyone responds in the same way. Constructive criticism may not always be received positively, even though this is the intention. Most people take it as a personal attack and may respond with an insult or harsh criticism, often at the moment. No one enjoys receiving a negative comment or feedback. When employers or managers must call an employee to review their performance, they often "sandwich" the comment about something they've done wrong with two other positive items, in a three-part discussion, such as the following example:

Step 1, the first comment (on a positive note): "You are great with the customers, and you're well-liked in the store."

Step 2, the second comment and item of concern to be addressed: "Sales have been slow, and we appreciate your efforts, but we need to see stronger results."

Step 3, the third comment, also on a positive note: "You are always punctual and ready to engage, so with a bit more strategy, I'm sure you can pull up those numbers soon!"

By using the above technique, a supervisor or employer can effectively get their point across without making the employee feel inadequate, or as though they are being "picked on." This method can save the problem of being accused of favoritism, which removes the focus on the negative. This example clearly shows how a negative incident or report can be framed as a concern and with other, more positive attributes too.

We can accuse other people of our flaws. This practice is called projection, and it can deflect our insecurities and faults to other people, even where there is no basis for them. It can inflate a bad situation to a much more explosive argument and cause more damage in the long term. Often, statements are made that can't be reversed or taken back. It can be challenging to mitigate the damage or insult once it happens. When we speak too soon, it's a defense mechanism. We can trigger this in other people when a specific topic or subject is discussed, causing them to react negatively because of their lack of knowledge or experience. If you are competent at evoking such a response from someone, they are easily affected and sensitive, even when they are not the target in any way. In general, it's best to avoid making a snap remark or comment that could lead to negative reactions later. When someone makes the same comment, it becomes an emotional response, which can lead to giving you the upper hand or control of the situation. The other person may feel they need to redeem themselves or "make it up" to you. For example, consider the following scenario and how it can impact someone in this situation:

A customer in a retail store that sells home décor may comment on how they would like to coordinate new furnishings and draperies in their house. A salesperson responds with offering a custom interior design service where a consultant will visit the home and make recommendations on specific styles and products. The customer initially feels offended, thinking that the remark hinted that they could not design and choose their furnishings. While this was a dispute, the salesperson takes a step back and doesn't respond except apologizing for the misunderstanding, then offers further assistance to answer questions about products if needed. The wrong approach would be to meet on the defensive and accuse the customer of being unreasonable. This would only inflate the situation and guarantee that the business would be taken elsewhere. By giving that space and time to reflect, the customer would have time to reconsider the comment and realize that it began with good intentions.

What we say can hide certain aspects of who we are, but in doing so, we may also reveal deep-rooted fears and envy that can cloud our judgment. It is important to regulate our emotions in a conversation, especially where a business or a formal address is required. On the other hand, cultivating an appropriate emotional response from the other person, such as a connection to safety and security for their family, is a good way to increase the chances of involvement and connection. Once you become aware of your fears and anxieties, it is easy to project them onto other people, though this can result in mixed results; either the other people will relate to the same concerns, or they will dismiss them and move on. If you insist on using the same focus on these fears and anxieties, this will only highlight your worries and further distance your chances of connecting with others who do not relate in the same way.

Becoming aware of your fears and anxieties is the right way to understanding how we can avoid projecting onto other people. Many people will avoid coming to grips with their inner fears and phobias because it is one of the most unpleasant experiences most of us encounter. It is because we equate acknowledging our concerns with facing them, even when we are not prepared to do so. It can be a much more complicated process for some people than others, depending on the level of fear and anxiety they experience. For people who have PTSD (post-traumatic stress disorder), anxiety, and other related diseases, this process may require professional assistance and guidance for the best results. For many people, the idea of admitting they have fear is a frightening realization, even if they are aware of subconsciously. This process is something many of us work through gradually, though it can be helpful and liberating in many ways too:

- Admitting your fear doesn't mean you have to face it, unless (and until) you are ready.
- Knowing your fear is an act of bravery because it means you can recognize its power over you and decide how you want to handle it.
- You become more self-aware about yourself and how it relates to the way you communicate with other people.
- Once you are fully aware of what makes you afraid, you can avoid projecting these same fears onto other people. This realization will significantly improve the level of connection

and communication you have with other people and allow you to listen to them more clearly.

When we focus on our relationships with others, it is not an easy task, especially where some bonds are strained and hard to improve. This realization can also impact the way we approach new relationships and how effective we are in connecting with others. Making new connections is all about first impressions. Still, soon after we make that impact, our relationship can quickly deteriorate if we practice some of the same mistakes in the past that may have ruined connections. We also need to recognize the importance of our most considerate efforts and skills even though some people will simply not connect with you, and you'll have to accept it. In some situations, there is no resolution but acceptance. What we learn from our relationships with some people can help us understand them (and others) much better in the future.

When we understand the way relationships develop, we can improve how we communicate to get what we want. If someone sees us only aiming at pursuing our interests, they will be less apt to help or get involved. Often, they will want to know if there is something in it for them. Not only is this a reasonable expectation, but it is also human nature. How reluctant would you be to put yourself on the line for someone unless there was some benefit or advantage in return? Even where there is altruism in your intention, most of us are careful and guarded when approaching a person or situation that may involve some risk. At a minimum, a show of reassurance or a return in favor can make a compelling case. From this perspective, it is important to keep in mind when using your skills of persuasion or manipulation. Even where the other person doesn't stand to benefit, it is vital to make a case to buy into your idea.

Learning to accept ourselves fully is another crucial step in reaching your goals. You cannot effectively convince other people to take you seriously and persuade them unless you feel the same about yourself. This means fully accepting who you are and understanding the importance of self-esteem. Even where we may struggle to gain an advantage in certain situations, it matters most how much confidence we present. When some people lack confidence, they may project a false sense of ego, which may not always be convincing. Furthermore, they may become easily agitated or upset when their tactics become ineffective, and they begin to take the outcome personally, even when this is no fault of their own. By making a point of improving your sense of self, this will shine through all your efforts and make your goal of persuasion much smoother in more situations.

Many people struggle with guilt and regret. These are two of the most harmful characteristics that will impede your progress, especially if you are a risk-taker and aim to win. There is no point in feeling regret about a past decision, though many people hold onto these moments, which fuels guilt and regret. When you accept that certain decisions were made and cannot be undone, this isn't easy to digest. This is challenging, especially if there were tragic or dire consequences as a result of the choice. For some people, turning down a progressive job offer or leaving a good relationship behind can become sources of regret later. It's important to realize that while these events shape our life, either for better or worse, they can also serve as lessons that can improve our decision-making in the future. When you consider your past and fall back on feelings of guilt and regret, remember the following points:

- The past cannot be redone, but you can learn from it. Some of the best lessons in life are learned from experience only, even if they are hard to swallow.
- You can make peace with your past and realize that while you cannot change it, it does not have to control you. You can make better choices starting today.
- Leaning on your past blurs your focus on the present and the future. No one will take you seriously if you continuously refer to past mistakes and regrets. This story will sound like someone who lived a tragic life with no solution. Alternatively, your goal is to build confidence and assurance that you are greater than your mistakes and headed towards success so that what you say and do will be more convincing and believable.

How you present yourself to the world says a lot about you. Sometimes, our perception of ourselves is vastly different from what others see in us. We may see our presentation as seamless and confident, while others see uncertainty and mixed messages. It's always important to assess your strengths and accept your weaknesses. When we experience self-awareness, it is a humbling experience, but it can also serve to build your confidence from a new starting point and allow you to sharpen your skills as a negotiator. This development is effective in its use of many skills

74

associated with dark psychology that you can employ to your advantage. Focusing on confidence should be your primary goal. In making these improvements, you will also become more self-aware and learn the motivations behind your actions and understand better what you need to do to improve yourself and your chances of achieving your goals.

CHAPTER 8
Frequently Asked Questions

Question: How can you improve NLP techniques to guarantee they will work to your advantage in situations where the other person seems aware of you and is not receptive?

Answer: There is always room to improve your skills, which is an ongoing process that takes time. Some people will naturally adapt and use the cues to their advantage right away, but it can take time. If you find that your techniques are not getting the results you want, then take a break from the situation (and the person) and try a different approach. Some people seem resistant to change and may not be subject to the same influence as someone else. Choose your "target" or the person/people carefully, as some people are more comfortable to persuade than others.

Question: Is hypnosis one of the best ways to influence someone, and how can it be used in practical situations?

Answer: Hypnosis is an exciting practice, but it is not always practical in its application. Unless someone is interested in being induced into this state, they are already under your influence, at least in part, and more likely to listen and follow what you want. In situations where hypnosis is not available, a suggestive state of mind can be invoked by repeating certain words or concepts throughout a conversation. If done skillfully and subtly, you may gain the interest of someone and hold their attention span longer to influence them more, though this varies from one individual to another.

Question: Is manipulation considered less ethical than persuasion?

Answer: By its definition, manipulation is considered deceitful and less ethical than persuasion, though there are reasons why a person would use manipulative techniques in certain situations. Manipulation can be seen as having two sides: it can give someone the power and ability to get more out of life, or it often means that someone else will not benefit or maybe "tricked" into doing something they did not want to. On the other hand, it can be a method used as a last resort, when conventional, more direct purposes are not successful.

Question: How can dark psychology work on someone successful in using the same techniques?

Answer: Not everyone uses the same strategy or techniques, which means you may have an advantage if the other person is not as well versed in specific tactics. For example, if you learn and practice neuro-linguistic programming principles, and know how to read their cues and gestures, this will give you the advantage. It's always best to observe first, as not everyone is easily persuaded or manipulated. When you evaluate your reasons for using dark psychology, make sure you choose the person or group of people carefully.

Question: Aside from sales, business, politics, and advertising, what other industries or professions use dark psychology or similar manipulative techniques on people?

Answer: This varies from one field to another, and while some professions are well known for their persuasive techniques, such as sales and politics, this can vary in consistency and the level of how these practices are employed. Professions in the arts and entertainment industry are widely known for their use of persuasion, with many people using NLP techniques in this field. Live performers can use their fame and influence to persuade their audience. Some are open about this, including magicians and people who use hypnosis as a form of entertainment. Executive-level positions and careers that demand a strong personality and ability to exert influence over others, including attorneys and people who advance quickly in large corporations, often have developed skills in dark psychology to get what they want for themselves and or their clients.

Question: If someone suspects you are trying to manipulate them, should you stop entirely or take another direction?

Answer: The answer to this question largely depends on the situation and how serious you are about getting results. It also depends on how well you can gain their trust (or regain it, if lost). If someone asks if you are trying to "force" or convince someone to decide, ask them if they are interested. Give them the impression that you want to work with them, not against their best interests. If they believe you, there is a chance they are prone to persuasion, but only if they are leaning towards the same direction. If a person accuses you of using manipulative techniques and the situation turns hostile, it is often best to abandon the whole situation. Keep it civilized and apologize for the misunderstanding, then move on. There is no point in pursuing a position that will not offer any benefits to you. In a serious situation where there is too much to risk, giving up is the best option to consider. This action will help you avoid potential problems or backlash later.

Question: Am I responsible for someone else's outcome if I successfully convince them to decide in my favor? What repercussions should I take to avoid legal or other problems later?

Answer: Firstly, never engage in a situation with the potential to put you at significant risk. If the potential harm outweighs the benefit, abandon the task, and move on to something more attainable and reasonable. Know your target and get comfortable with the scenario before you engage. Moving too fast for your own pace can cause grief later, especially if you lack the confidence and ability to deal with difficult situations that may arise. All conditions carry an element of risk that you should expect every time you plan your next move. For some people, the greater the risk, the more likely they are to engage because they enjoy the thrill and don't mind taking chances. These individuals are seasoned with the skills of manipulation and know how to talk their way out of many scenarios. For the beginner, taking a big leap too soon will put you at too much risk and is not worth the potential benefit. It is best to always begin in your comfort zone, and work with what you know first, then build and expand from there.

Question: Why are some people naturally more charismatic and persuasive than others?

Answer: Some people have a natural ability to persuade others and make a favorable connection right away. It can be an inherited personality trait and or something they were always good at since childhood. For others, this takes time, and results will vary from one individual to the next. Most people will find that applying practical methods, like those mentioned in this book, can effectively improve your chances of making a good impression. This option is a good start and allows you to build your techniques further. Realistically, it is essential to realize that not everyone will have the same results. However, making the strive towards improving your techniques will go a long way to secure a better rapport and relationship with people and increase your chances of success.

Question: How can I read people effectively when they are good at hiding their true feelings and intentions?

Answer: Many people are not aware of how their hidden agenda has the potential to be discovered. Sometimes, just a few simple observations and the ability to notice them at the right time can unveil a lot! In the same way that dark psychology can improve your techniques with gaining influence and control over other people, the same criteria can be used to determine when people are using the same or similar tactics against you.

Question: Is it safe to assume that almost anyone can use dark psychology at some point in life, or are there people who will never use it?

Answer: Most people use some form of persuasion or manipulation to get what they want. This is true even when they are unaware of it or don't like the idea of it. A child will use one parent against the other to gain a favorable answer, often causing a rift between them, while gaining a reward of a toy or something else they want. Even the seemingly most benign techniques are a form of exerting a form of control or force over another person to coax or persuade them in your favor. In adulthood, these tactics grow into more sophisticated plans and agendas, though there are many other ways to get more out of someone or something by using simple methods and being observant. Many people fail to get what they want because they don't take the time to assess the situation and offer them. Once they realize the benefits and how easy they are to obtain, the rest of the process is how willing you are to use persuasive techniques that may shift into a more potent form of control or manipulation. Everyone is capable, to a degree, of getting what they want, provided they are willing to take some risk and make use of some useful techniques along the way.

CONCLUSION

Dark psychology is a fascinating subject of study and offers a wide range of skills that you can use for your benefit in many situations in life: networking and gaining the approval of your colleagues and community, getting the promotion, or securing a date with someone you may find unattainable. In learning the techniques associated with the "dark" side of our mind, we not only gain more insight into what we want as individuals from a more primal and basic foundation, we learn about how other people respond to these tactics. Even in the most skilled people who have mastered persuasion and manipulative techniques, there will always be room to learn and develop what you learn today to improve your chances tomorrow. There are always changing circumstances when one method or technique will work better over another. You'll learn in the process, and with experience, your ability to work magic will only improve with time. As a beginner to the world of dark psychology, it is essential to keep the following points in mind when developing your skills for achieving your goals:

- Greatness comes with practice and consistency. Don't let a few bad experiences ruin your overall direction and goals. When you are ambitious, this takes a lot of time and commitment to work in your favor. Keeping the momentum from the start will ensure your improvement over time.
- Always be persistent. Some situations may warrant abandoning if they become too risky, but for most people, persistence is the key to getting what you want. One of the biggest reasons people fail is because they are not focused on their success. After a few attempts, they no longer feel the same confidence to continue. This pitfall will only ensure failure because of quitting, though keeping despite setbacks is the best option, even if you don't see the immediate advantage.
- Give yourself time. Don't rush into situations too quickly, and apply your newly learned techniques until you feel genuinely comfortable giving them a shot. It means taking the time to get to know the target and situation you wish to pursue, and what options are available to you. Are you looking for an opportunity that may need some light persuasion, or is it a more complex scenario where more robust manipulative techniques are required? Don't jump

into a situation that is too tough to handle when you're still learning your methods. Also, remember that standard procedures are only valid when they are used by someone who can exude confidence and apply them well. Make sure you are ready and comfortable first, and try some milder forms of influence first, such as developing charisma and charm, as these can go a long way before persuasion begins.

- You don't have to be the expert, and sometimes, even the most experienced masters of persuasion make the mistake of targeting the wrong person or situation. One of the best teachers is experience, and this will happen time and again. When you become familiar with how people communicate and what they mean, this will provide a powerful direction to control more situations to your advantage. Learning the traits of dark psychology can serve to give you an opportunity, though it's also important to continuously learn and observe over time, to improve your chances of using the tools of influence and manipulation to your advantage.

The world of dark psychology offers a way for you to get the most out of situations that you may not have felt in control of. Imagine having the ability to gain more influence over people and situations that were previously unthinkable or unattainable. When you unlock the mystery of the human mind and discover how people deceive each other, this becomes a vital way to understanding how we can use certain techniques to increase our knowledge of each other and take greater control. By learning the skills of various practices such as hypnosis and NLP, and/or simply observing more about the people and circumstances in life, we will have a greater opportunity to get the most out of life.

DESCRIPTION

Dark psychology is a fascinating field of studying the mind, and how we can use various techniques in both subtle and significant ways to get what we want. Persuasion and manipulation can become a powerful set of skills that can benefit you in various scenarios and situations where they are effectively used. Tapping into your charm and charisma can also lead to securing strong connections with people and influencing them for many advantages, from personal relationships and building social circles to improving your prospects at work and beyond. In this book, you'll gain a new perspective on how to read and understand people, while learning more about which techniques and habits you'll need for success:

- The basics of dark psychology and how it can work for you: understanding the underlying principles and how they can work for you
- How dark psychology is effective and who uses it today in business, politics, advertising, and within your network of friends and colleagues.
- An introduction to neuro-linguistic programming (NLP) and how this practice can sharpen your ability to control and influence people
- The value of hypnosis and why it is a powerful way to invite a stronger influence and effect over people
- How to develop charisma, charm, and build a rapport with anyone
- Manipulation and persuasion: the similarities and differences, and how to know which technique to apply for best results.
- Reading people and how to decipher their true intentions, from body language and non-verbal cues to gestures and subtle, hidden signs that indicate what people want

Learning the advantages of dark psychology and what works best in various situations will give you the tools you need to succeed on your terms, and by using other people and their influence to move ahead. Imagine harnessing the ability to decode the true nature of your boss, coworker, or colleague to unleash hidden agendas that you can use to your advantage. By learning simple yet effective ways to read other people and understand their real intentions, you'll be able to take the upper hand and gain more control and knowledge than ever before. Furthermore, you'll avoid many pitfalls of becoming prey to someone else's manipulative tactics by knowing exactly what to look for and avoiding the negative impact of these situations, while boosting your chances of gaining the advantage over others.

If you are new to the world of dark psychology, there are many ways to learn and benefit from simple exercises of observation and proactive behavior to develop more elaborate and engaging ways to create a strong level of influence whether you know the person well or meeting them for the first time. There are many intriguing and exciting ways that we can connect with people for our advancement and pursuit of more in life, from closing your first sale to developing a relationship with someone you may never consider possible. There is a strategy for everyone to succeed on their terms with the right attitude and ambition.

MANIPULATION TECHNIQUES

Discover How to Analyze People Through Mind Manipulation, Psychological Techniques and Body Language

Judith Dawson

INTRODUCTION

Manipulation—it is something that everyone thinks they have an opinion on, but no one quite realizes what the truth of the matter is. Is it good? Bad? Always negative? Can it be used positively sometimes? All of these are hard to answer for most people—it becomes difficult to understand where the lines can be drawn. The truth is, like with just about anything else out there, the truth to manipulation is that it can be good *or* bad. It can be used to influence people to help them become better, or it can be used to destroy someone's very sense of being.

Manipulation is used widely throughout the world. We use it when we negotiate and haggle, believe it or not. We use it when we attempt to persuade someone else to do something. Even the most honest salespeople out there are manipulating you in their own ways—and this is just fine. It is okay that they are doing so—it is okay that they have their own ways to do what they do. It doesn't necessarily make them good or bad—it just means that they are using manipulation.

Ultimately, the word manipulate refers to the act of molding something else. You manipulate clay; for example—you use your hands to change the shape. The word itself comes from French, which drew from Latin's *manipulus,* meaning handful. This is precisely what manipulation is as well—it is a sense of molding someone else into what you want them to be. Now, whether that manipulation is innocent or not depends primarily on what follows after the fact. Do you manipulate in hopes of getting your way when you are trying to do something? Do you do so in hopes of bettering the other person? The intention behind the manipulation matters—and that intention can vary greatly from person to person. Depending upon how you choose to utilize it, your own manipulation of other people can vary immensely. You just have to figure out what you will do with it when you do spot it.

Imagine a situation in which Alice tells Bob that she really likes his steak so much better than her own. She really loves how, when he cooks it, the salt crystallizes just right, and there is a beautiful sear on all sides. Alice raves and raves about the steak that Bob makes— and Bob then decides to make some steak for the two of them. Is this manipulation? Technically, it is—it is actively attempting to alter the way in which someone else is behaving. You are intentionally trying to make it a point to take over the situation that you are in. You are forcing your own personal point through attempting to influence the way that the people around you see the world.

It is technically manipulative, but is that as harmful as someone who may be attempting to groom someone else into being a lifelong victim? Probably not—we have all sorts of different manipulative situations in which sometimes, people choose to engage with people in ways that are not actually helpful. We have these situations in which sometimes, people are controlled for nefarious or selfish purposes, and we also have situations in which we are influenced for other reasons. A doctor may employ manipulation to gain compliance with medical treatment; for example—they may insist that, if the patient does not comply, they are likely to die long before their children come of age, for example. Technically, this is manipulative, as we will be addressing shortly. Just because something is manipulative is not inherently problematic- the problem comes with the intent that follows. If you choose to manipulate other people, you can do so without much of a problem, even ethically, if done for the right reason.

This book is here to begin to delve into the idea of manipulation of other people. Though traditionally wielded by people with darker, more sinister mindsets who only wanted to use and abuse people to get ahead, you are able to make use of many of these techniques in day-to-day situations in which you will be able to get the most out of them. You will be able to see that ultimately, you are able to do better with those that you engage in. You will be able to begin working on how you are able to better influence those around you in hopes that you will be able to make a real difference. We will be taking a look at several different examples of manipulation to begin to understand how it can be used and why that matters. We will spend the time to consider what manipulation is, how it works, and who cares to use it. We will be taking the time to look at all sorts of other information as well, such as what to expect with forms of manipulation. From emotional manipulation to persuasion and form NLP to taking a look at brainwashing and hypnosis. We will be exploring several different options, all of which have been used to some degree or another to control people around you. You may not feel like you are very susceptible, but the truth is, the human mind is surprisingly fragile. The human mind is surprisingly easy to influence and alter, and because of that, unsuspecting people can be highly influenced by ease if someone knows what they are doing.

Now, if you are not the kind to care to manipulate others, that's fine too—you can take a look at how you can begin to recognize these different tactics for what they are. As you continue to learn about the information that you will be reading within this book, you can begin to understand what is used to manipulate other people. You will be able to recognize what it will take to begin to control those around you, or you can choose to take that information with you to begin recognizing when others attempt to control you instead. Through this information, you should be able to understand what it will take to combat manipulation on yourself, or you can choose to utilize it to your advantage.

Keep in mind that manipulation is not always bad—you are able to persuade someone to take a look at purchasing an item that you identify as being the right one for them, even if they disagree at first. You are able to learn to negotiate like a champ with ease as well—learning to negotiate is something that typically involves body language, persuasion, and a bit of NLP sprinkled in for good measure. When you learn to use these methods and put them together, you are able to create a powerful force that people would be hard-pressed to challenge. When you continue to negotiate against other people, you are able to begin to take charge.

As you read through this book, make sure to keep an open mind. Some of the information might seem far-fetched at times—you might not think that you actually do have the control that you have over people, for example. Or, you might find that you are uncomfortable with the information that was presented to you. However, this information is good to have. If you do not know how to protect yourself, then you are going to struggle to spot the people that are the most likely to cause harm to you. With effort and some practice, you will be able to begin spotting what it is that you ought to be looking for. If you are able to do this for yourself, you will see that you are able to ultimately succeed.

Now, let's get started at diving into the world of manipulation. Hang on—it's going to be a wild ride.

CHAPTER 1
What Is Manipulation?

Manipulation itself is something that a lot of people fail to properly identify and label. It is something that is meant to be relatively easy to understand—it is as simple as influencing the reactions that someone else has, controlling the perspective that they have over what they are doing at any point in time. If you are able to recognize the influence that you have over those around you, you are able to begin to control how you engage with the world. You are able to begin to have better control over yourself as well, and that is highly powerful. If you want to be able to control how those that are in your vicinity behave, then you are in the right spot.

Within this chapter, we have a few primary objectives. We will set out how to define manipulation. We will be taking a look at how to begin identifying the ethics that go into manipulation, as well as how to understand who it is that manipulates other people. Finally, we will take a look at why people manipulate in the first place. This chapter will serve to set the foundation for everything else—you will be able to see precisely why so much of what is out there in this book is as sinister as it is just by seeing the people that the manipulation is based upon. As you read through the chapter, you should end with a better appreciation for what manipulation is and how important it can be.

Defining Manipulation

Psychological manipulation is a form of social influence that is designed to allow for the changing of the behaviors or the perceptions of other people through your own actions. Typically, the manipulative actions are indirect, deceptive, and sometimes even underhanded to get what is desired. Usually, as well, the entire purpose is to advance the interests of the individual interested in manipulating in the first place. It typically comes at the expense of someone else, but the manipulator typically does not care.

Social influence itself is not always a negative thing—it is something that allows for social pressures to mold us into what we ought to be at any point in time. If you want to make sure that you are working with yourself to better who you are, you will want to engage with your own social influences to help yourself begin that change. Doctors and nurses, for example, will influence our behaviors that directly influence our health and wellbeing. Family and friends might urge us to change up how we engage with other people. The social influence that we have is generally perceived as harmless within certain circles—it can be rejected or accepted and typically is not very coercive. However, manipulation usually goes a step further with the coercion that exists.

Is Manipulation Always Bad?

Of course, this begs the question of whether manipulation is something that is always, without fail, bad. The truth is, it is not. It is something that is actually surprisingly flexible. Manipulation itself is more akin to a tool than anything else. While it tends to be deceptive or underhanded, sometimes, that can be justified if the ends are the right ones. If you are able to get through a situation and get that proper end result, you know that what you are doing is going to be worth it. Certain situations simply make sense for manipulation to occur, such as in that example of a doctor or a nurse attempting to influence the treatment that someone gets. With this idea in mind, it becomes important to take a look at how you are able to define your own boundaries. How far do you want to go? What are you willing to do—and what are you not willing to accept? This information will help you. However, remember that manipulation itself is no worse than a gun or a knife. Used in the right context, both can be the difference between life and death—sometimes, you need a gun or a knife for protection, for hunting, or for general survival. Sometimes, they are just nice to have on hand for something. And, sometimes, they are used for nefarious purposes that would not help anyone.

Recognizing that manipulation is very similar in the sense that it cannot really be good or bad, but it can be accepted or rejected, you begin to see that ultimately, it is something of a tool. It really is just a tool that you are able to use to influence the minds of those around you, and if you get good at using this particular tool, you are able to find that your own skills and abilities are made dramatically better with ease.

Who Manipulates Others?

Manipulative people, especially those who are maliciously manipulative, have mastered the art of deceiving everyone around them. They have become highly skilled at being able to change who they are, how they engage with the world around them, and what they do at any point in time. They might seem to be perfectly nice from the outside, but oftentimes, this is entirely fake. They are there to draw their victims in. They want to make it clear to their targets that they are someone that should be trusted. After all, trust is one of the primary components to being able to manipulate someone unless you intend to resort to the blackmail of some sort. Manipulative people are those who are not really interested in you unless you serve a purpose. They are there to gain control over people—they want to get their way as much as possible, and so long as you comply, they will allow you to continue on as if everything is relatively normal. However, if you don't comply, they tend to snap. They play the victim, or they lash out. Again, remember that at this point in time, we are primarily discussing the manipulators that are likely to be malicious in intent over all others.

Typically, the malicious manipulator lacks insight into how they engage with others, or they believe that the way that they have chosen to approach a situation is the right way that will meet their own needs above all others. They may be controllers or abusers. They do not care so much about what other people need—they want their own needs met. Boundaries? They have no regard for them! You tell them to keep their distance or to do something differently? They will pretend that they have not heard them, or they will simply completely override them, period. They will crowd you and push you about, willing to take control of the situation and you by all means—even if that means intimidation in hopes of getting you to comply.

They also tend to avoid their accountability—the skilled manipulator is never at fault, and they will always find a way to blame everyone else for the problems that they face. They see nothing wrong with refusing to take responsibility, but they will absolutely hold other people accountable as much as possible. They may even try to make their own problems yours as well in hopes of shirking off the responsibilities as simply as possible.

Typically, the most manipulative of all fall into what is known as the Dark Triad—they suffer from three dark traits that make them highly dangerous and ruthless. They do not care about hurting others because they have little regard for empathy or maintaining relationships. The Dark Triad consists of:

1. **The Narcissist:** The narcissist is someone suffering from narcissistic personality disorder. This person oftentimes finds themselves being incapable of empathy, struggling to see the world realistically, and will work to make themselves

the center of attention at all costs. They work to make sure that they get the world that they want above all others and that world places them solely in the limelight. To the narcissist, no one can be better at anything than they are—otherwise, there is some egregious harm that must be dealt with.

2. **The Machiavellian:** The Machiavellian is someone who believes that the ends will always justify the means. To them, people are little more than tools to help them arrive at their final destination. They don't care so much about ensuring that they are well-liked—they just want to make sure that they get whatever it was that they were seeking, no matter what the cost may be. They will work as hard as they can to make sure that they get what they want, and they do not care how many people they have to step on to get there.

3. **The Psychopath:** Finally, the last person to consider is the psychopath. This is someone who simply does not care about other people. They do not care what it will take to get them what they want, and they will use people just because they can. These people lack any sense of empathy and do not seem to have any qualms with hurting those around them if it means that they will get whatever it is that they are looking for.

Ultimately, this dark triad becomes important to understand—most of the study of dark psychology, which the contents of this book heavily overlap with, will take a look through the eyes of these people with the Dark Triad. They tend to take what those on the Dark Triad would do and use that as a sort of emulation for how to get through everything. When you take a look at how these people tend to engage with each other and with those around them, you see that these people are dangerous, and they don't care what it takes to get what they were looking for in the first place.

Why Do People Manipulate?

Ultimately, people manipulate for all sorts of reasons. Some of the reasons are simply because of the fact that they fall into the Dark Triad. Others are forced into it. Others still have all sorts of reasons that they may choose to turn to manipulation for themselves and those around them. It is often that there are these very real reasons behind it, and when you begin to understand what they are, you realize the truth—that the manipulators that are out there are highly powerful.

Now, let's take a look at those common motivations for manipulators—understanding them would help you immensely with becoming capable of identifying those that may be manipulating you or those around you.

- **They have a need to push their own agendas:** Oftentimes, manipulators do so because they do not care about what happens to other people—but they do care about what happens to themselves. They find that they have something that they need to push, usually advancing their own personal gain, and they are willing to do so, even at a cost to those around them. They do not care—they just want to get what they want without having to deal with the waiting.

- **They have a strong need for superiority:** Often, you are able to see that manipulative individuals do engage in manipulation because they want to make themselves feel powerful. They want to make sure that ultimately, they are the ones that get to deal with what they do. They want to make sure that those around them recognize that they are the superior ones, and they will push at all costs to make it happen for them. They will not hold back.

- **A need for control:** Sometimes, the motivator for the manipulator is simply getting control over a situation. Being in control of who those around them are is a great way to make sure that they are able to stay on top and that control is earned through learning to influence and manipulate others.

- **A need to feel power over others to boost self-esteem:** Sometimes, what is desired is a boost in self-esteem. When someone's self-esteem is lacking, it can be hard for them to really feel like they matter in the world. For some people, they make themselves feel more powerful and boost their self-esteem by making it a point to control others. They see that they have that control over someone else and that boosts how they feel. After all, it is difficult to be able to control others—they have to trust or hold you in a high enough regard to allow you to control them, and that allows for a bit of an ego boost as a result.

- **Boredom:** Sometimes, people are just bored. They want something that they can do to help themselves boost their own personal entertainment, and they choose to play a game. They are not really trying to hurt anyone or get ahead—they just want to play a game to alleviate that boredom and grant them the entertainment that they are looking for.
- **Covert agenda:** Sometimes, there is a genuine covert agenda underlying everything. This is a theory that not everyone is willing to accept—but it is there. Oftentimes, people see the world around them as a barrier to complete a covert agenda. Sometimes, for example, elderly people are targeted for the covert agenda of scamming them out of money because they are usually not as technologically savvy, and they also struggle to really understand everything else that goes into scams these days. When they get a phone call from their granddaughter, crying that she just got arrested a few states away for something silly and that she needs money ASAP, they tend to be swayed just by virtue of the fact that they care about their children or grandchildren. That is a covert agenda to steal the funds from elderly individuals because they are deemed less likely to notice in the first place.
- **An inability to feel emotions:** Sometimes, the individual who manipulates others simply does not realize that they are doing so. They may struggle to, for example, feel their emotions or make sure that they can do better. They feel nothing that would usually hold people back from manipulating those around them, and without those underlying emotions, they do not really realize that they are manipulating in the first place. Or, they may find that they are so busy trying to convince themselves that their own emotions are false that they wind up hurting others instead.
- **Lacking self-control:** Some people are simply impulsive—they wind up being terrible at being able to control themselves and any of the urges that they have. With those impulses in place and no empathy to help them to hold back, these people wind up reacting in ways that become manipulative to others.

Of course, there can be other reasons to want to manipulate someone else as well. However, those are the most common and are the ones that you are the most likely to find yourself encountering as you go off on your own journey.

CHAPTER 2
The Subconscious Mind And The Key To Manipulation

Did you know that you are not actually aware of everything at all times? Even when it feels like you are, the truth is, there is a whole wide world out there, all of which is there to be explored and enjoyed. However, you are only enjoying those moments when your conscious mind states that you are, or if your unconscious mind decides that it will be a good time.

The truth is, the subconscious can be a bit tricky- it is that inner voice in the back of your head when you think. It is there to help you guide yourself or to make sure that ultimately, you do choose out the right situations. Your subconscious mind acts as a sort of automated feature in your mind—it allows you to work quickly and without as much regard to what you are doing at any point in time. Think about it this way—your subconscious is your autopilot. We all do things throughout the day that eventually become so habitual that it would be more of a detriment to have to think about every single action as we do them. The most common way to think about this is by driving. By learning how to drive, you have to do everything consciously at first. New drivers are terrified of getting into an accident because they still must work on how they move, what they do, and the way that they will put their feet on the pedals. Over time, however, the more that they do this, they commit the act of driving to their subconscious minds. This is why people can drive while talking after they have gotten the hang of things. They realize that they are fully capable of getting through what they do, and they embrace it. When they drive, they can do so effectively— all because their unconscious minds take care of it for them.

The subconscious mind has weaknesses; however—it is surprisingly easy to take advantage of, and we will be exploring this idea shortly. When it comes to the subconscious mind, you must be aware of this easily exploited weakness because if you do not take steps to avoid the problem, then you are far more likely to run into issues.

The Subconscious Mind

When it comes to the mind, the subconscious plays a few key roles. The subconscious is responsible for keeping you safe and alive. It is there to navigate the world without requiring your awareness. Unfortunately, the human mind is only able to focus and actually comprehend one thing at a time in any effective capacity. This means that, while you are reading, you are not really absorbing, consciously speaking, whatever is going on around you. You might be reading this book, and there could be people right behind you, having a conversation. You probably do not really catch the gist of what is being said. However, if something that they say doesn't sound quite right, or it is something that is directly about you or something relevant to you, you suddenly realize that you were paying attention all along. That's thanks to your subconscious mind.

Your senses are always working. They're constantly attempting to perceive what is happening around you. Even though you may not be consciously processing what the people around you are saying, you are still subconsciously recording it. Your subconscious mind then determines how to respond. If it is something important, it gets bumped up to your conscious mind. If it is not, then it is left to fall behind. This is imperative to note—when you pay attention to this, you start to realize that, ultimately, the way that your mind works is ingenious. You have the conscious part where you are able to focus, and your subconscious works as a sort of backup—it pays just enough attention to your surroundings to actively turn your attention there if necessary. This allows you to not have to waste conscious effort on everything you do—rather, you are able to only pay attention to what is pertinent at the moment.

Of course, this means that your subconscious is also out of your current awareness. You are not aware of it consciously because your conscious mind can only focus on one thing at a time. As you will see with many of the different options that we will be discussing, manipulation itself can happen within the subconscious mind in several different manners, all because you are unaware of your subconscious.

Manipulating the Subconscious Mind

When it comes to manipulation, then you are primarily targeting the subconscious. This is because your subconscious mind is what will pick up on your attempts to manipulate. The subconscious mind becomes capable of perceiving everything, but it also does not filter. Your conscious mind is not aware of what the subconscious perceives, and because of that, manipulation can occur easily. This is precisely how manipulation in the form of altering body language works—when you alter your own body language to attempt to

97

influence or control the other person, you also create a situation in which you are being perceived by the subconscious mind of someone else. That subconscious then alters the way that you behave.

Think about the last time that you did something without thinking about it. Perhaps you found yourself standing in the same position as those around you. Maybe you found yourself feeling small without really understanding why. This is due to the fact that you are ruled by the way that your body moves. You are controlled by the way that you tend to behave solely because of your subconscious mind. Because it is your subconscious mind's job to keep you safe and alive, it is constantly filtering out how you behave. It is always influencing how you approach situations and what you do. This is its downfall, however, and as you continue to read on, you will see why.

The reason behind the fact that the subconscious is so easily influenced is because your subconscious is responsible for emotions. This is why your emotions that you have will never fully be within your control. No matter how hard you may try, there is no way that you are able to tell yourself, "Yes, I am happy now," or "No, I'm miserable or angry or frustrated." You cannot simply persuade yourself to feel a certain way—you feel what you feel, and that's that. However, the reason behind this is because your subconscious creates those feelings that you have.

This is powerful for one specific reason—your feelings create actions. There is a cycle that is commonly accepted within psychology, particularly in cognitive psychology, in which your thoughts, feelings, and behaviors are all intricately linked together. Your thoughts influence your feelings. Your feelings influence your behaviors. As a result, your behaviors also have a role in reinforcing those unconscious thoughts that you had. This all works together to create that cycle. Manipulation works by changing up one of the three rungs in the cycle—it works by causing some sort of shift in thoughts, feelings, or behaviors, which then changes the rest of the cycle as well.

Most commonly, manipulators will attack either thoughts or feelings—both of those are the easiest points of contact to control the other person. It is simple to make someone think a certain way if you know what you are doing, and this will be a primary focus when we take a look at neuro-linguistic programming. Alternatively, controlling emotions also comes easily if you know what you are doing—it just takes you being able to control yourself well enough to actually get the effect that you are looking for. For example, you might alter someone's emotions by controlling how you talk to them or how you present yourself. One way that we will discuss in persuasion involves appealing to the emotions of other people. Ultimately, through making it a point to influence the emotions of others, you then trigger their behaviors to be different as well.

Manipulators are experts at this. They are skilled at finding the weak point in figuring out what needs to be done. When you look at this with the idea of hijacking one's thoughts, feelings, and behaviors, you realize that ultimately, that power is there. You realize that the power that manipulation has runs far deeper than you probably thought possible. As you read through this book, you will begin to see it all play out—you will learn about how these interactions work for you and how you are able to use them in your own favor.

CHAPTER 3
How To Use Manipulation

When it comes to being able to use manipulation, there are a few different factors to consider. If you want to manipulate someone else, you must meet three primary criteria that all must come into play. You must be willing to conceal your own aggressive intentions, as well as be well aware of the vulnerabilities of your target. Finally, you must also be ruthless. All of this comes together to create the effect of manipulation that you are looking for in these situations. When you are able to make use of manipulation, you usually will follow through with certain methods of control, and there are usually very specific vulnerabilities as well.

Within this chapter, we will be addressing this idea of how to use manipulation, as well as what it will take to control people. We are going to be focused on several of the most common methods of control, along with the most common vulnerabilities that are targeted to exploit. When it comes to being able to control other people, it takes effort and an understanding of the underlying information as well. If you know what you are doing, however, you will be able to thrive at controlling the situations that you are in, no matter what kind of situation that may be.

Conceal Aggressive Intentions

First, you must make sure that your aggressive intentions are hidden. Typically, manipulation is considered aggressive because of the fact that it is usually attempting to control other people. This, in and of itself, is aggressive and must be managed well. If you want to be able to manipulate other people, one of the best ways of doing so is by making it a point to remain hidden. This is because most of the time, manipulation only works when the other party is unsuspecting.

Think about it—if you know that someone is intentionally trying to manipulate you, are you going to want to do what they wanted? Probably not—you will probably try to do anything in your power to prevent a repeat of what is happening. However, if you do not know that the other person is acting in a calculated manner to try to maintain control over you, you aren't going to go out of your way to stop it. This is why being able to control through the subconscious is so important—when you work to control someone from their subconscious mind instead of from their conscious mind, you are able to get further just by virtue of the fact that you are working to remain hidden.

Know Vulnerabilities

Additionally, it becomes imperative to understand and recognize the fact that the manipulator, in order to be effective, will need to have a solid understanding of the vulnerabilities of their target. They must make it a point to understand which of the psychological vulnerabilities will get them the best possible result and how they can go about it. When it comes to being able to spot those vulnerabilities, you realize that ultimately, you are able to begin to figure out how to control other people. Imagine that you know that someone is vulnerable to being left to feel like they are worthless. If you know that when they feel worthless, they start to wonder how they can make themselves do better and therefore feel better as well. When you consider the idea of being able to encourage people to feel in very specific manners, you will then be able to take advantage of them if you choose to do so. If you want to be able to control people around you, you must first begin to figure out how to chip down the defenses of the other person. You have to work toward bringing down those walls that surround people, so you are able to create your own network. You do this, so you are able to make sure that you will be working with strings that are powerful. In doing this in this manner, you show yourself how you are able to get control of a situation.

Be Ruthless

Finally, if you want to be able to use manipulation, you must be ruthless. You can't let your own guilt eat at you for being dishonest or for doing something for yourself. The best manipulators are those that are unafraid. They are the ones that are willing to do just about anything if they want to be able to get what they want. They are the people who have no problems being willing to do what it will take to succeed. This ruthlessness doesn't have to mean that you are cruel or evil—it just means that you are willing to do whatever it takes to make sure that you get your way. It means that you do not have to feel bad for what you do—you just have to do it. This can be something that many people grapple with if they want to learn to get that control over people as well. However, it is something they will have to do if they want to succeed. If they want to be able to succeed at manipulating people or controlling people, they will need to be able to actually have that ruthlessness that will allow them to do so without feeling so bad about it.

Methods of Control

Ultimately, when it comes to controlling people, there are several different methods that work well. All of these methods of control are fantastic ways for manipulators to control their victims. As we go through these different methods of control, think about them— these will be relevant as we go through the future chapters as you begin to discover what it is that you will do to influence others.

Positive reinforcement

First, there is the usage of positive reinforcement. To use positive reinforcement is to attempt to convince the other person to continue to do something by rewarding the behavior. Positive reinforcement is what you get when a desirable event or stimulus is presented after a behavior in hopes of getting that behavior to continue again in the future. Think about the idea of training your puppy by providing them with a treat every time they obey you or do something that you want them to do. By rewarding the behavior with positive reinforcement, they see that they get something that they want when they do what you want. There are all sorts of different ways that this can play out, such as with someone who chooses to love to bomb their partner in hopes of making them want to continue doing what they want. Positive reinforcement usually includes methods such as:

- Apologies
- Approval
- Attention
- Expressions
- Gifts
- Money
- Praise
- Recognition
- Superficial charm
- Superficial sympathy

Negative reinforcement

Negative reinforcement refers to the idea of removing a negative situation as a reward for behaviors. You are taking away something unpleasant when you see the other person do something that they should have. For example, if you were to ground your child for not cleaning his room, negative reinforcement would be allowing your child to then leave the room upon completing the task. You are putting your child under pressure in hopes that they will be willing and able to do what it will take to get them back on track to doing what they need to do. Negative reinforcement usually involves you creating an unpleasant situation in the first place, though this is not always a requirement.

Intermittent reinforcement

Intermittent reinforcement is one of the strongest because it creates doubt and fear. When you utilize this particular form of reinforcement, you run into other problems—you run into a situation in which you find that being hot and cold actually makes you seem more attractive to the other person. The idea is that because you are pleasant to be around sometimes, the individual will seek you out, and will double down and persist when you are not. This is the same sort of logic that has led to gambling addictions—it is the idea that you are able to get what you want if you know what you are doing, and that is highly powerful. If you want to be able to control the situation around you, the best thing that you are able to do is make it a point to make yourself unpredictable.

Punishment

Punishment is the intentional reaction toward someone to discourage behavior through negative events. It happens when you intentionally inflict discomfort or pain onto someone else in hopes of being able to control them better. You want them to feel like what they have done is unacceptable or is something that ought not to have happened, so you make it a point to take things out on them. Punishment typically can be just about anything, but some of the most common forms include:

- Crying
- Emotional blackmail
- Guilt trip
- Intimidation
- Nagging
- Playing the victim
- Silent treatment
- Sulking
- Swearing
- Threats
- Yelling

Traumatic one-trial learning

Finally, when you use traumatic one-trial learning, you are making it a point to use explosive anger, abuse, or attempts to establish dominance over a situation. It could be verbal and emotional, or it could be physical. When it comes to being able to utilize this, the victim is conditioned or trained rapidly to walk on eggshells around the manipulator for fear of exposing the problems. The victim does not want to end up in a situation in which they trigger the anger because they know what will come next—they know that ultimately, they will find themselves hurt or upset if they dare to frustrate their manipulator. They obey out of fear, and this allows for compliance to be held rather simply.

Common Manipulative Techniques

When it comes to the most common techniques that exist, most manipulation tactics fall into one of several simple categories. These different techniques are incredibly effective over time—they are able to keep people down, so the manipulator is able to do what he or she wants. If you learn to understand these different methods, you will start to recognize the patterns—you will see that ultimately, you are able to control people, or your eyes will be opened to the truth, so you are able to protect yourself as well. Let's go over some of those most common forms of manipulation now:

- **Bandwagon effect:** In using this method to manipulate, manipulators make it a point to gain submission by pointing out how everyone else uses these items or that everyone else similar to them does something. It is meant to feed on peer pressure to make sure that the individual wants to move forward with something. This is commonly used to try to influence an individual to do something that they may not have wanted to do in the first place.

- **Brandishing anger:** When manipulators make use of their anger, they use it to attempt to keep their victims intimidated so that they can continue to maintain control over the situation. They want to shock the victim into being submissive again, and the manipulator will do this primarily through attempting to appear angry, even though they may not actually be frustrated at all—they just want the benefits from the anger. They often use this as a manipulation tactic to make sure that those around them are kept back. It helps them to avoid confrontation and allows them to continue to hide the truth because the victim will be too startled and, therefore, too timid to do anything about it.

- **Covert intimidation:** When using this, the manipulator will put the victim on the defensive because they will use threats to try to keep them down. This is because, when the victim is on the defensive, they have no choice but to try to defend themselves, and that means that the attacks on the individual also come to a screeching halt.
- **Denial:** During denial, the manipulator entirely refuses to admit to something. They either try to obscure the truth, or they have other methods that they use to make sure that the truth does not come out. As a result, they are able to retain their own element of control over the situation.
- **Diversion:** In this instance, the manipulator refuses to give a straight answer to a question and instead attempts to get around it. The manipulator will most commonly attempt to redirect toward a completely different topic entirely.
- **Evasion:** This is similar to diversion, but in this case, there are often vague responses given, or the responses are irrelevant or rambling. The goal is to distract instead of diverting.
- **Feigning innocence or confusion:** The manipulator will sometimes simply play dumb—they refuse to be acknowledged as the problem entirely. They would much rather make it clear that they are not the true problem—they want to deny that they knew that there was a problem there in the first place, and through doing this, they are able to maintain their semblance of innocence that they wanted.
- **Guilt-tripping:** When using guilt trips, the manipulator wants to convince the victim that they are selfish or that the victim is not actually deserving of what they have. This is done to make the victim feel guilty for gaining compliance.
- **Lying by omission:** This form of lying occurs when a significant amount of the actual truth of the matter is hidden away or obscured for some reason. This form of lying hopes to leave out detail without offering it up—though the lie never actually took place, they also made it a point to avoid offering up that information when they should have. When questioned, they most often object, saying that they weren't asked to tell anyone anything, and because of that, they are not at fault.

- **Lying:** It is hard to tell when someone else is lying if you do not know what to look for, and though the truth may come out eventually, it usually does so when it is too late to get anything done about it. One way to start cutting down the chances of being lied to is to make sure that you understand what to look for-- learning the body language, becoming more stringent with yourself, and working to find a way to prevent yourself from being a problem are all great ways to make sure that you are not being lied to.
- **Minimization:** This particular behavior is denial, with a side of rationalization. When using this, the manipulation claims that their behaviors are not harmful because they were not actually serious. This is most commonly seen with telling people that something that was taken seriously is actually just a joke and that the people should not be as offended about it.
- **Playing the servant:** When the manipulator does this, they act as if what they are doing is hidden under the guise of just doing their jobs. They say that they are obedient or they are serving someone else—they cloak their own agenda in their service in an attempt to obscure what they are doing.
- **Playing the victim:** In this case, the manipulator attempts to revert things so that the victim is actually the attacker, while the manipulator is the one that has suffered. This is done to get the manipulator that pity and sympathy that they were looking for.
- **Projecting the blame:** When manipulators realize that they are going to be caught, they very quickly project the blame onto other people. Most often, they will attempt to make the victim appear to have done something wrong and make it so that the victim is the one that gets blamed. They will also claim that they were the ones wronged to further disguise themselves. This kind of thinking is meant to make sure that the victim is kept down. The most common way of doing this is to accuse the victims of being deserving of the abuse or paint the victim as the true abuser in a situation.
- **Rationalization:** When it comes to rationalizing something, the manipulator is attempting to make excuses for behaviors that are flawed to some degree. They may, for example, attempt to explain away an action that raised red

flags as being culture, or they may try to make you feel like you are the crazy one for questioning something.

- **Seduction:** When a manipulator uses seduction, they use charm, flattery, praise, and their own support in hopes of getting a victim to lower their defenses. In doing so, they are able to gain that loyalty that they were looking for, which allows for further control over the situation.

- **Selective inattention:** In this instance, the manipulator is attempting to avoid giving attention to something that may not support their cause or claim. By falling for this, you see that there are very real problems—the manipulator denies the problem by claiming that they were entirely unaware of the problem in the first place.

- **Shaming:** Some manipulators prefer the use of sarcasm and offensive comments in tandem to create doubt and fear in the individual to allow for further control. The manipulators in the world prefer this tactic because shame can be triggered with anything from a glance at each other to actually saying things that are meant to keep the victim down and afraid. Manipulators typically will use this to keep their victims from ever actually crossing them to make sure that they maintain that control they are looking for.

- **Vilifying the victim:** In this tactic, the victim is put on the defensive while also making it a point to hide the aggression behind what the manipulator is doing. At the same time, the manipulator makes it sound like the victim is the one causing problems—the victim is painted as the true manipulator or abuser in this situation.

Common Vulnerabilities

Ultimately, there are several vulnerabilities that you must consider when it comes to dealing with manipulators. These are the easiest points in which someone can manipulate someone. If you are looking for a target, this list would be your starting list of figuring out who can be controlled, how they can be controlled, and why it matters. Consider all of these different exploitable vulnerabilities yourself:

- **The need to please:** This is the desire that some people have to make sure that everyone around them is getting what they want or need. It is that feeling that they must make sure that everyone is happy and that the happiness of others falls on their own shoulders.

- **Addiction to approval from others:** Some people find themselves entirely caught up in whether or not they can get approval from others that they are looking for. They find that they are entirely stuck needing to get that approval from others, and they will do anything in their power to make that happen.
- **A lack of assertiveness:** Some people simply cannot bring themselves to say no. They may try—but their own inability only brings them down. They find themselves stuck, unable to find a way to communicate their disagreement without feeling like they are vocalizing disapproval in a way that they should not have been.
- **Blurry sense of identity:** Some people simply do not have any real sense of who they are. They struggle with the idea that they can create either their own identities and that they have that power over themselves, and as a result, they are easy to take advantage of. All the individuals have to do is push that sense of identity further and further until it can be taken advantage of as a result.
- **Low self-**esteem: Another major problem that leaves people vulnerable to abuse and manipulation is the lack of self-esteem. When you lack self-esteem, you find yourself in a position where you do not trust yourself. You would rather trust just about anyone else over yourself because you assume that they will be in the right. You assume that they will be far more likely to know what they are doing, and as such, you trust them over yourself.
- **Emetophobia:** This is the fear of emotions—particularly those that are negative. It is a fear of either expressing negative emotions or of being on the receiving end of negative emotions. When you fear the emotions of yourself and of those around you, you are able to run into significant problems that must be addressed. This can really hold you back if you do not know what you are able to do to begin to mitigate it.
- **Naivete:** When the victim is too naïve to realize that they are being taken advantage of, they make very easy targets that can be used and controlled. Manipulators know this,

and they look for naïve individuals who may be willing and able to provide this for them.

- **Overly conscientious:** People who are highly conscientious care immensely about other people, and they give them far more consideration than they really should be. When it comes to being willing to give the manipulator the benefit of the doubt, there can be serious problems. There can be issues with all sorts of things if you don't know what you are looking for. In particular, you are able to expect to see that there are several problems when you are constantly giving other people the benefit of the doubt, but they are not willing to return the favor.
- **Low self-confidence:** Another thing to consider is the idea of low self-confidence. Manipulators see this as a mark of an easy target, and if you find yourself falling for this, you will realize that ultimately, you run into all sorts of issues that you will have to address. Your self-confidence, or lack thereof, could lead to situations in which manipulators find themselves taking total control.
- **Overthinking:** Sometimes, real vulnerability is the tendency to overthink things. The victim may find that they constantly attempt to understand why something happens the way that it does or how to better cope with it. The more that this is done, the more likely that it is that there will be other issues as well. When you consider this, you will see that these targets tend to allow for everything to pass by because they get so caught up in wondering whether they are overthinking the issue or not.
- **Emotional dependency:** Some victims are simply willing to risk everything for those around them. They will find themselves feeling as if they must make it a point to get along with those around them. They choose to find ways that they would be able to continue to make sure that they are closely tied to those around them, and that means that they are oftentimes willing to forgive just about anything if it means that they get to maintain their position that they are in.

Typically, manipulators will look for an assortment of these traits or tendencies in their victims—they are able to spot these weaknesses, and they take control of them. They want to be able to utilize this tendency toward being able to control those around them, and they will do so in just about any way that they can manage to justify.

CHAPTER 4
Emotional Manipulation

Emotional manipulation is highly insidious—it is something that leaves no visible marks on its victims. It can leave people feeling controlled, confused, and sometimes, even as if they are worthless. It can slowly but surely destroy everything about someone else, holding them down and back. Have you ever found yourself feeling something that you could not quite explain? It could have been the result of emotional manipulation. Likewise, have you ever made it a point to figure out how you could begin to influence the emotions of those around you? This is also a form of emotional manipulation. Within this chapter, we are going to address a few key concepts: We will first spend some time identifying and defining what emotional manipulation is. We will then go over several different types of emotional manipulation that are designed to take charge, take control, and get people doing what the manipulator wants them to do. If you learn to pay attention, you are able to start to see how this works—you are able to realize that you are more capable of figuring out how to control people than you may initially think. Or, you may learn that you are able to spot this form of manipulation with ease as well.

What Is Emotional Manipulation?

If you are going to utilize emotional manipulation, the first key consideration to remember is that emotional manipulation can undermine relationships, hurting the victim. This is something that you must consider—is this something that you are willing to do? Will you pay the price for this? If so, then keep reading. If not, no harm is done.

Emotional manipulation is designed to make sure that people are able to influence the emotions of someone else. Technically, by that definition, even a baby crying for food could technically be deemed emotional manipulation—it makes the mother want to stop the baby from crying. However, in the scope of this book, we are looking at acts that are deliberately self-serving for the manipulator—the acts are those that will directly influence and control the people and will lead to the reactions that the individual is looking for. It is commonly done in order to get one's own needs met, or sometimes, to achieve goals. However, so long as the manipulation is designed to influence the emotions of someone else, it officially falls under this bracket, and that is something that you will have to consider as well. You must make sure that you are in a position where you understand what you are doing before you begin—because this form of manipulation can cause serious harm if you do not know what you are doing.

Love Bombing and Devaluation

This first method of emotional manipulation that we will discuss is the idea of love bombing and devaluation. This exists in a cycle— the cycle involves first strongly addicting the target to the manipulator, and then occasionally making the target feel as if they do not matter or as if they are irrelevant. When you do this enough, you run into a situation in which the target, who is being fed intermittent reinforcement, grows closer. They try harder.

Typically, love bombing happens at the beginning of a new relationship of any kind—the idea is that the individual, every time he or she comes over, will leave behind presents, praise, or general words of kindness. This typically is piled on far quicker than most people would normally be willing to accept—but you assume that it is genuine and move on. You accept the love bombs, and you enjoy them. You'd think that this is the end of this story—but it is not.

Ultimately, love bombing is that act of promising that affection at first, and then, devaluation occurs when the target is completely and utterly tossed to the side. The idea is that in doing so, the target is going to want to be right back onto that point of a pedestal that he or she wants to do. This sort of emotional manipulation can then be used to try to sort of entice the individuals to continue looking at it.

Fear, Obligation, Guilt

When you use Fear, Obligation, and Guilt, you are making use of their key feelings that you sometimes have. These relationships that you build are not built upon the right foundations to help, and they may even cause significant trouble if you do not know what you are doing. However, the truth is, these three emotions are highly powerful. Fear motivates people to avoid things that might be dangerous. Obligation works by making people feel like they have no choice but to comply. Finally, guilt is a powerful motivator that we have that tells us not to ever repeat something again.

When you consider this method, then you will be working to influence and control the emotions of those around you. You might try to intimidate the individual, or you may have something else to say to them that will help them begin to fear the situation. Then, you may find that you choose to encourage a sense of obligation. You may do something for them, so they feel obligated to do the same when the time comes. This is perfect in getting what you want, as we will be addressing shortly.

Finally, let's talk about guilt. Guilt is the feeling that is there to drive people to never repeat the same mistakes again. It is there to remind the individual that they must change to be in a better situation. It is there, so you do not continue to do things that will hurt you or those around you.

When you put all three of these together, you have a very compelling source of information and control that you are able to continue to use if you need it. By taking this control for yourself, you are able to begin to control other people as a result.

The Silent Treatment

The silent treatment is not usually thought of as emotional abuse, but it Is time to identify what is meant when you are talking about the silent treatment. The silent treatment is this point in which one or two partners refuse to speak to the other one. Maybe they disagreed on where to go out to dinner and ended up insulting the taste of the other. Neither party was able to find an agreement that was satisfied, and as a result, they voted nothing. They did not upvote or downvote. They were not there to cause problems with the election or to do anything other than carefully but subtly do their thing.

The problem with the silent treatment is that it is, well, silent. It involves refusing to speak—it involves being willing to simply not communicate due to selfishness or due to not wanting to get involved in something. However, it is also highly effective if you absolutely must get a job done. It will help you to do that much at the very least.

To use the silent treatment, all you have to do is remain silent when someone else is talking to you. By remaining silent and refusing to engage, you are utilizing this method.

Gaslighting

Finally, the last method that we will briefly look at in this chapter is the idea of gaslighting. Gaslighting is the idea in which you will attempt to convince someone else that they cannot perceive reality around them. The idea is to make them feel so concerned, so out of power, and so out of touch with everything around them that they begin to rely on their partner's perceptions as well. At first, it starts out innocently enough—you might notice that something is not where you left it, or you may find that you are questioning what you did and your partner says something else. However, one thing has been found: This form of manipulation can be highly dangerous.

Using this begins with building up trust and then carefully working your way to ensuring that you have that control that you are looking for. Through gaslighting, you will start to deny small things. If your partner says they left their keys on top of the table, perhaps you find them on the floor next to the counter instead. You slowly do this over time—usually over a week or two—and you slowly but surely manage to mark off every instance of what you are doing and how you need to change. You will start to accept what the other person wants you to do and you will have no problems simply deferring to him or her. Over time, this eventually erodes further into what you know as manipulation today. When this happens, you see the fullest effects of the gaslighting, and as a result, you may find yourself in utter control of someone else, or you are able to get and maintain that control as well if you know what you are doing.

Either way, gaslighting becomes something that is dangerous if it is in the wrong hands. Gaslighting is highly important for just about anyone to have an understanding of, and without it, you will struggle. Keep in mind that while at first, this is little more than a table game. However, over time, it gets bigger and bigger. You could see that your target will take your word as a rule and will always follow. Alternatively, you could wind up biting off more than you think you are able to chew.

CHAPTER 5
Mind Control

Do you wish that you could influence or control someone else? Have you ever wondered if you could just find some way to influence what other people are doing with ease? Do you wish that with a simple snap of your fingers, you could properly influence the way that you engage with other people? While you cannot simply take control of someone else in the sense that you may be thinking, you do have the ability to heavily influence the way that they think. You are able to begin to influence how people behave by controlling those thoughts in their own way. All you have to do is be willing to see it your way and go forward.

In this chapter, we are going to take a look at a few different ways that manipulators are able to control the minds of those around them. Being able to control someone else's mind is something that is highly powerful. It is something that you are able to utilize in all sorts of different ways that will allow you to do so much more. Through being able to do so, you will find that you actually have far more control than you realize. Controlling the minds of everyone around you will allow you to take that control that you were looking for. Being able to understand what is going on and when it is happening, you will be able to see precisely what you need to do to take control.

What Is Mind Control?

First, it is important to note what mind control is *not*. It is not something that will grant you utter control over what someone does. You will not likely be able to simply tell them, "Go do this now" and get good results. However, what it will do for you is grant you that ability to better understand what they are doing and why they do things the way that they do. You are not just magically controlling people, as the name may imply, but you will be able to influence how that person sees the world around them. When you learn how to utilize mind control, you are able to make sure that you speak or act in ways that will help you directly learn how to influence them. You learn what it will take for you to make sure that they are behaving in ways that benefit you.

You are controlling thoughts and feelings in hopes of influencing behaviors when you utilize mind control, and by doing so properly, you will find that you are able to actually make major progress in how you engage with people. You are able to start to convince them of what they need to do and how they should do it. You are able to make sure that they know what it is that you need from them so that they can feel like you do understand them. You want to make sure that ultimately, you are talking to them in ways that will motivate them.

Mind control works primarily because your thoughts will influence your feelings, and your feelings will influence your behaviors. In particular, we are talking about unconscious thoughts here—the thoughts that you are entirely unaware of. Your unconscious or subconscious thoughts are those that you are not actively thinking, but that influence you nonetheless. In particular, when you have these thoughts, they are controlling you from the background without you having to do anything at all. When you utilize this process, you are doing so because the unconscious mind is constantly paying attention to the world around you. Your unconscious mind will always naturally tune in to things around you so that it can pay closer attention to the world around you without you having to also be aware of it. It allows you to save that awareness for when you really need it. Keep in mind that your mind is something that should not be taken lightly. If you are going to control the mind of someone else, then make sure that you do so tactfully.

With that cycle of thoughts, feelings, and behaviors, you ought to see that controlling the minds of those around you becomes quite simple for you. You simply must learn to pay attention to that never-ending cycle. This loop will help you to influence people: It allows you to start to shortcut—to take the thoughts of someone else and apply them to what you are doing. If you do this enough, you will get great at spotting what you must do.

Types of Mind Control

When it comes time to identify how mind control works, you must also understand that there are several different ways that you are able to use it. If you want to be able to control the other person, you will usually use one of the very predictable forms of mind control to make sure that you get that power over them. When you have that, you are able to start to actually piece it all together and make it happen.

Isolation

The first method that we will consider is isolation. When people are in isolation, they will suffer. We are a social species, and with that comes the inherent need to crave connection to other people. We naturally require other people to be around us so that we can thrive. We are not meant to be kept alone without other people. When you do isolate someone else, you start to control who they are around. Through being the only point of contact that person has, you are then able to start directly and significantly influencing their mind. This is relevant here—if you want to control other people, you must make sure that you are taking control of how they see themselves as well. This is precisely how cults tend to take control—they isolate their followers so that they have no choice but to accept what they are doing and being stuck with where they are. They start to believe everything that is said about them, and over time, they accept the cult ideology, completing the process.

Through isolating someone else, you are able to wear them down easier over time. You are able to start instilling that doubt in that person—they will start to think that no, they are not fully capable of thinking or acting accordingly. When you do this, you are working to properly take control of the other person.

To isolate someone, you must first be able to develop a good relationship with them. You must be able to get into a position of trust so that you are able to start to take that control in the first place. You are able to do this in several different ways, such as utilizing your body language to become an authority figure or working to make it sound like you are the individual's only ally in the situation, which is a tactic that you will also see during brainwashing when we get to that chapter. The more that you do this, the more likely you are to successfully get the other person to listen.

Essentially, through isolating them, you are able to develop enough trust that you will be the primary point of control. If they need an opinion about something, if you have isolated them from everyone else, the only place that they can go is to you. That is something that you are able to use to help yourself in control and in power in this situation. As you do this, you slowly plant the seeds of what you want them to be and how you want them to think. The more that you manage to succeed at this, the more likely that you are to actually maintain that mind control that you are looking for. To isolate someone, you have a few different options:

1. Physical isolation in which you restrict the movements of the other person to keep them within your grasp so that you are able to control all external resources and maintain complete control over the situation and individual.
2. Mental isolation, in which you make them feel like they are alone, whether they are or not. You could be blocking phone calls or intercept letters or messages. You send the idea that nobody cares and that they are truly alone, making them easier to control.
3. Censorship, in which you start to limit the influence of the outside world. You make it so that there is as little contact with the world around them as possible. By doing this, you are capable of influencing the only direct contact that person gets to the world.

Criticism

Criticism is an attempt to indirectly control everything around the other person so that they feel like they are ground down and want to give in to everyone else. When it comes time to be capable of controlling the other person, you want to make them feel like everything that they do is under complete scrutiny. This is perfect for taking control of the other person. Through your ability to nit-pick at the other person, criticizing them at every chance that is afforded to you, you start to build that sense of doubt within them. They start to feel like they are the ones that are problematic instead of you. They assume that you are not the problem because they naturally trust you and what you are doing and saying. The more that you are capable of covertly criticizing them, the more likely that you are to get that desired result that you were looking for.

For example, imagine that you want your partner to get a better job. You might mention that you wish that he had a job that made more money. You may choose to mention that you wish that there was a way that you could afford something more. You might point out how your friends' partners are starting to make more money, and you wish that your partner was as well. You want them to feel like they are in a position where they are going to be criticized for what they are doing and how they are doing it. The more that you are able to push this point of criticism, the more likely that you are to find a way to cause problems. There are all sorts of ways that you are able to do this, but it all boils down to simply using shame to control the other person. You are trying to make the other person feel bad about themselves so that they are willing to give in to what you want. You make them feel like the only way for them to fix their problem is if they actually make it a point to change up the entire situation and do what you wanted from them in the first place.

Peer pressure

Through peer pressure, you are able to also control people. Remember, no one wants to be alone, and no one wants to feel as if they are stuck or unable to get past a situation because of how they behave. They want to fit in—if they feel like they do not fit in, they often want to comply with fixing the problem as soon as possible. This means that through utilizing peer pressure, you are able to actually sort of influence how people choose to behave. Through this sort of influence, you are capable of getting people to do just about anything. All you have to do is make sure that you put things in the light of you want them to do something because it is what everyone else is doing.

You could, for example, make sure that the individual is primarily surrounded by only other people that do what you want them to do, utilizing isolation as well as this sort of peer pressure to control the other person. You could also simply appeal to statistics that prove the stance that you are taking in which people have no choice but to admit that yes, things do have to go a certain way.

Repetition

Finally, you are able to also make use of repetition to control the other person as well. When you make use of repetition, you will be able to start putting ideas into the mind of the other person to control them. Remember, the mind is constantly listening, and because of this, you will be able to identify how the mind always pays attention to its surroundings. This means that over time, your unconscious mind will absorb information that could be used to control it as well. This is information about, for example, what your mind is doing at any point in time. You could also control the other person by repeating the same message over and over again in different contexts. This is effectively subliminally attempting to assert control over someone else—you are counting on them, not realizing that their unconscious mind is absorbing that opinion little by little. The more that this is done, the less likely that they are to properly fight the point in the first place. This method, of course, requires tact and some degree of covert attitude to the whole situation. You must make sure that you are working well to make sure that they will not pick up on the repetition, but that it will be absorbed in other ways.

Think about it—you could be making it a point to repeat a point about a book or movie or even an unpopular opinion about something. The more that you reiterate this point, whether they are aware of it or not, the more that you will start to plant that message to them. Think about how often we look at what is happening around us. Consider just how often we tend to do things in a certain way because of sheer repetition as well. The more that you recognize and tap into this, the more likely that you are to successfully plant that idea in the first place.

CHAPTER 6
Neuro-Linguistic Programming

Next, let's take some time to go over neuro-linguistic programming. NLP is a common way in which you will be able to start influencing the minds of other people solely because you are capable of understanding the relationships between the body and mind. Through tapping into those relationships, you are able to start to work out truths and even heal from traumas over time. It is highly potent, powerful, and is even easy to learn. The initial purpose behind NLP was to provide something that the average person could learn to teach themselves or those closest to themselves about how they can move on in life or change themselves to be successful. Now, while it has the potential to be abused, NLP is also something that can really do a lot of good for people, especially if they regularly see a practitioner. It becomes something that they can utilize to help themselves, and they often find that it is highly influential as well. If you want to make use of NLP, you must recognize the truth: That there are these massively important ways that you are able to interact with the world.

Keep in mind that, though NLP and mind control shares some similarities, this is not actually the case. NLP is meant to be built upon a solid relationship with the other person—it is meant to create rapport through mirroring with the other person. This idea is that the mirror neurons between yourself and the other party will be strong enough that you feel that intense chemistry. That chemistry is known as rapport, and rapport will help you immensely in life. Rapport will help you to tap into what you want—it will allow you to properly influence and control the way that the other person is thinking so that you are able to influence and control them as well.

Just like with mind control, you will be utilizing the same cycle of thoughts, feelings, and behaviors. You will be influencing the way that the people act through influencing their unconscious thoughts. The idea is that your conscious and unconscious minds are not able to fully communicate with each other- they both exist separately from each other. However, through actions, they are able to communicate. Your unconscious mind is able to create feelings that influence your behaviors, and when you use NLP, you are influencing the unconscious mind of someone else.

What Is NLP?

Designed so anyone can do it without requiring psychology training, NLP is a method of influence in which you are able to communicate with the unconscious mind of someone else to influence their behaviors. It effectively allows you to use your own body language and actions to directly influence the unconscious mind of someone else so that you are able to then see precisely what they are doing. Through this indirect attempt to influence the other person, you then get that control. You learn to control them through controlling their unconscious mind. This is done through vocabulary, actions, and more. Little by little, you will use your own actions to directly influence the other person.

All that matters is that they must sense what you are doing. You are able to influence any of the senses—sight, sounds, taste, smell, or touch can allow you to directly influence the mind. You are able to make certain tastes or smells trigger certain thoughts to control a reaction, for example, or you could also make it so that the individual is going to respond to certain words a certain way. This sort of conditioning allows you to take control of that person with ease. All you have to do is make sure that you are in full control of the situation.

NLP works because people have a way that they all see the world, and that way is very distinct. That way that they see the world is something that can be altered. Remember, how you see the world and interpret it is subjective, not objective. That subjectivity is something that is easily altered. You are able to start to change the mindset that other people take about something relatively simple. All you have to know is how to present it to rewrite that map of reality. Once you actively tap into their mind and change how they choose to behave, you are able to maintain control over the other party. The more that you do this, the easier it will become. All you have to do is encourage the thought, feeling, or action that you want them to begin using, and everything else will follow.

Mirroring, Rapport, and NLP

Before you are able to begin to utilize NLP, however, you must first develop a rapport with the other person. This is the reputation that you hold with the other person. It is the measure of the relationship that you and the other person share—it is the way that you both communicate in an effective manner. When you and the other person have a rapport with each other, you are on good terms—you are on the same page, and you will also be working together more. This is something that can be seen at a glance when you see other people wandering around with each other. If you want to identify people with good rapport with each other, you must take a look at how they engage with the person that they are with.

When people have a rapport with each other, they both mirror each other. Mirroring refers to what happens when two people follow each other's movements. Imagine how you see friends walking alongside each other at the same pace, with their steps happening at the same time. They also may take a drink at the same time, or they might move about together. If one person touches their head, the other will do so as well, or when one person shifts, the other follows. This happens because when we view someone doing something else, similar areas in the brain will go off as well. However, the part that goes off is not the same part that causes you to do the same thing. It is the part of your brain that helps you to empathize with them. This is what works well to allow for people to relate to others.

Mirroring is something that happens naturally most of the time, but it is also something that you are able to force as well if you do not have the time to start developing the relationship with others. If you want to make sure that you are capable of triggering that rapport from other people but are short on time, you have options. Perhaps one of the most common ways to do so involves taking a few minutes to mirror the other person first. Because the unconscious mind is always paying attention, being able to mirror someone else first cues to them that you are mirroring them. This then triggers this concept of reciprocity—their body will naturally follow along as well, and that is highly important as well. When that happens, you start to see that they are actually far more interested in following along. This is because they almost feel compelled to do so- -they feel like they are required to follow along even though they may not actually have that relationship set in stone yet.

Mirroring, then, is one of the most important skills that you are able to develop if you hope to be capable of managing the way that you interact with other people. If you want to be able to control others, then you must make sure that you are able to influence them your own way, and that includes being capable of watching how you engage. Mirroring follows a few simple steps when you need to do it, all of which are incredibly easy to manage.

1. **Attention:** It all begins with attention. Make the other person the center of your world, so you are able to properly develop a pseudo-relationship with them. You want to be fully convinced that you like them if you want them to like you in return. See them as the most important person for you to talk to at the moment, face them, and make eye contact as you listen to them.

2. **Mimicking:** Next comes the mimicking stage. Now, many sources will tell you to follow the body language, taking their poses and movements, or drinking when they drink, but if you are not naturally following each other, they are much more likely to see that you are doing it at the moment and that can cause you problems. If they catch that you are deliberately following their body language, they will be much less likely to like you—they will simply think that you are weird or untrustworthy, and that is highly problematic. Instead, mimic their vocal cues. This will allow you to follow their nonverbal communication without being visually obvious. Due to differences in the way that voices sound, they are much less likely to notice if you are simply following along with their body language than if you were doing something else. This means you should follow how they speak. Listen to how they tend to pace themselves. Pay attention to the tone and the excitement level in their voice. Match it and keep pace with them. Their unconscious mind will notice, even if consciously, they entirely miss the point.

3. **Seal the deal:** The third step requires you to seal the deal by tapping into the punctuator. The punctuator is something that is used by people whether they realize it or not. The punctuator is the way that you will accentuate what you are doing at any point in time. Some people have a phrase they use when they are speaking. Other people choose to move a certain way as they engage with someone. Some people still waggle their eyebrows, or they smirk or smile. This is important—and you should be able to figure out what it is that they are doing every time they do. Listen for their punctuator, and when you figure it out, you will then need to copy it. You want to copy it for them the next time they are getting ready to say something. By beating them to the punch, you are able to seal the deal. They may not catch that you are copying them, but they will feel like

you are paying close attention to them, and that will help to trigger them to feel that connection as well.

4. **Test:** Finally, all you have to do is test it. See if that connection is present there. You want to make sure that they have that connection with you before you attempt anything else. Try moving slightly—you could move yourself to the left and see if they shift to the left as well. You want to see if they are shifting around with you so that you are able to begin to tell what they think. If they follow along with you with small movements, then there is a good chance that they have that rapport built with you. That is a great sign for you—that means that you have succeeded. If not, you will need to start over and try again. If you cannot get through to them and convince them to follow you after a few attempts, then you will need to let go of the idea that you will actually get them to mirror back.

Following these steps will help you to develop that connection with other people so that you are able to influence them over time. When you have that mirroring established and they are following your actions, you will then be able to influence them simply by tapping into their body language.

Anchoring With NLP

Anchoring is just one of the many ways that you are able to utilize NLP. Anchoring is effectively allowing yourself to connect to other people. When you anchor someone to something, you will be able to influence them to have a conditioned response every time that they do something. Effectively, you will be able to move or prevent something from someone, and they will then trigger that response every time. This will allow you to control the behaviors of someone else, and it can go in several different ways. You could, for example, start by encouraging someone to feel like they must listen whenever you hold your hand a certain way. This is a good way to convince people to follow you if you are looking for obedience. You could also choose to utilize anchoring for yourself to remind yourself to stay assertive or to make sure that you are calm if you are an anxious person. Through anchoring yourself with a certain item, action, or thought, you will be able to calm yourself down as well. This is imperative if you want to be able to influence other people. Thankfully, anchoring is incredibly simple—you just have to follow a few simple steps.

1. **Identify what you want to condition:** First, you must figure out what it is that you want to trigger whenever you want it. Do you want them to feel a certain way? To concede in a confrontation every time? Figure out what it is.
2. **Identify your stimulus:** Then, you must also know what it is that you want to use to trigger in the other person. You want to be able to figure out how you are able to convince them to do what you need. It could be that you use a certain movement. You might want a certain word that you will use.
3. **Trigger the reaction:** To begin the conditioning process, you must first find a way to make them think or do what you were thinking. For example, imagine that you want to make someone apologize at a whim. You want to do something that will make the other person apologize to you. Maybe you make it so that they bump into you. Then, they will naturally apologize.
4. **Use the stimulus immediately after:** Then, as soon as you get that reaction, it is time to use the stimulus. You may use a certain hand gesture as they say that they are sorry.
5. **Repeat:** You will need to repeat this several times, but with time, you will start to conditionally respond to them. Over time, you will start getting them to apologize just by moving that certain way in an argument or when you want them to do something.

This works because you simply condition them over time, little by little, to get them to properly follow along with you and what you are doing or what you want them to do. This is perfect if you want to condition someone else, so you are able to control them.

Weasel Words With NLP

The last form of NLP that we will look at here is the utilization of weasel words. This will allow you to communicate with people and convince them to do things just by how you speak to them. By changing up the way that you speak to the other person, you will be able to properly influence the other person. This is a great option for you if you want to know how to speak to people to get the reaction that you are looking for.

Effectively, you are leading the thought processes that someone else has by making sure that you phrase your questions and statements in a way that will naturally start to influence their thinking or worldview. This is effective in many ways. If you want to be able to tell them what to do or how to do it, you must make sure that you do so in an effective manner. You must make sure that as you engage with other people, you do so in a way that will allow you to help everyone involved. You must make sure that you think carefully about what you say so that you are able to convince them properly.

You start with questions that naturally lead to what you want them to do. For example, instead of asking if someone would like to buy something, you ask when they will buy. This shift in language makes their mind believe that buying is already determined and that they have nothing to think about. Rather, they must buy because there is no other choice. This is perfect to shift the focus, altering the unconscious mind, which then assumes that it *is* buying just because of the way that you spoke to it. This is perfect if you want to be able to convince people to purchase things or if you want or need to influence how people engage with others. You could also use language such as:

- After you...
- As you...
- When you notice...
- You may experience...
- You may realize...

With these ambiguous phrases, you slowly influence the mind of the other person to accept and appreciate what you had to say. Through doing so, you allow yourself that utter control over them, which is highly influential for you. The more that you are able to do this, the better. That vague ambiguity will grant you the ability to ride on plausible deniability without them realizing what you are doing at any point in time. There are really just a few key points to remember when you choose to use weasel words: You must make sure that you speak something that is a command with the tonality that shows a command as well. Through doing so, you should get them to unconsciously absorb what you say to them.

For example, maybe you are trying to sell a car to someone. You may say, "When you buy this, you will notice that it runs really well." Notice how you embedded that command—"You will." This is the key here. What you have said is all things considered, quite simply not offensive. However, you will also notice that there is more to it. The very way that it is phrased is done in such a way that it will influence them.

CHAPTER 7
Body Language

Body language is another powerful way that you are able to use to compel people to follow along with what you want them to do. It can be used in several different ways to get people to influence and control what they want or need. When you are able to understand the body language of other people, you are able to start to figure out what it is that you are able to do to influence other people as well. Because we see the body language of other people when we approach them, or when they approach us, we respond to it. This is why being approached warmly by a friend or family member can leave you feeling good while being approached by someone that is not so kind will actually lead you to feel nervous or even defensive or aggressive.

Through tapping into body language, you are able to start to influence other people as well. They will see what you are doing, and they will then alter their own behaviors to reflect upon that. You will influence other people simply by knowing how other people's minds work, once again tapping into that cycle of thoughts, feelings, and behaviors. When you are good at paying attention to these things, you are able to start recognizing just how likely it is that you are able to alter how they behave and what they do.

Remember, body language is powerful for a reason. We rely on it heavily, and we utilize it without ever thinking about it. However, you are able to also willingly and intentionally tap into it to begin to change how other people behave as well. This is imperative—the more that you alter how you respond and engage with other people, the better. This allows you to better influence how you are seen and helps you to be in control of a situation. When you are able to assert yourself as the dominant one, you are able to usually influence how those around you engage with you. Through doing this, you are able to then maintain control over the other person. You are effectively looking to use your body language to influence how the other person engages with you in hopes of being able to control them more thoroughly than you otherwise would be able to. Through doing this the right way, you maintain that air of confidence and control.

Leading Body Language

When you want your body language to lead other people, there are a few key ways that you are able to move yourself to ensure that the other parties around you see yourself that way. You do not have to do much to make yourself appear confident enough to be a leader—you just have to engage the right way to maintain that degree of leadership. If you play your cards right, you will find that you are highly successful at that level of influence that you are looking for. To lead with body language, consider the following to change your own movements to take control:

- **Maintain eye contact:** By ensuring that your eye contact is maintained, you are able to be confident as an individual. However, you must hold that eye contact with the other person in a way that is gentle rather than dominant or overbearing. You are not trying to come across as intimidating—you are looking for a way that you are able to relate to them more clearly. You are showing them that you listen to them and therefore, are giving them the attention that they deserve without being intimidated or uncomfortable by the process.

- **Stand tall:** When you keep your body language tall and open, standing up with your spine straight and keeping your head level with the other person, you are seen as confident enough to be a leader. The key here is that you do not want to be looking down your nose at the other person—you want to ensure that you stay straight with them. If you are able to do this, you are able to maintain that semblance of confidence that you are looking for.

- **Release tension:** Make sure that you are not tense when you are looking at the person that you are trying to lead or influence. You want to make sure that the calmness that you exude shows the confidence that you have.

- **Maintain open body language:** To have open body language is to be capable of showing that you are open to being engaged with by people around you. It is a relaxed body language that shows that you are non confrontational and that you are willing to engage; however, you must deal with those around you. Make sure that you do not cross your arms or put something in front of yourself.

- **Use your hands:** When you talk with your hands, you show that you are confident enough to keep your hands visible at all times. Doing so helps you to properly engage with those around you. It also helps you to avoid falling into traps, such as fidgeting with your hands or hiding them in your pockets.

Dominant Body Language

When it comes to having dominant body language, you intimidate other people into following you instead of convincing them that they want to, the way you would with a leadership type body language. Through domination, you are able to control the situation in an authoritarian manner. To dominate a situation, you want to ensure that you are as big as possible to other people. You want to make sure that you are in control rather than anyone else, and through doing so, you show that you control it all. Consider the following body language:

- **Keep a wide stance:** When your stance is wider, you show that you are not afraid to take up space. When your stance is wider, you show that you are more dominant just because you do take up the world around you. You want to be as big as possible, and this is the best starting point.
- **Keep hands on hips:** By putting your hands on your hips, you make yourself larger as well. You are controlling how you are seen by making yourself puff up larger.
- **Head up with the chin high:** When you do this, holding your head up with your chin tilted out, you make yourself larger than they are. Through doing this, you look down at the other party, which makes them feel like you are larger or taller than them.
- **Spread your stuff out:** When you spread out all of your stuff, you start to claim the space all around yourself as well. Through doing this, you show that you are more dominant because you claim more than what is around you. When you do this enough, encroaching on other people's space, you are able to show that you want to take control.
- **Touch other people's things:** When you start touching other people's things, you start to declare dominance over them too. You show them that you are claiming ownership of things that you touch as you go.

- **Walk along the center of a path:** When you push yourself through the center of a path without making space for other people, you show that you are the dominant one. You make it clear that you will not move because you do not need to. This allows for that declaration of dominance without having to do much at all. When you do this, you show that you will not share space.
- **Stare at other people:** When you stare at someone else intensely, you will be able to declare dominance over other people. Through staring at people, you make them more uncomfortable, and through doing so, you are able to declare that domination.

CHAPTER 8
Persuasion

Persuasion is another way that you are able to take control of other people, and it will allow you to convince other people to do what you want. When you persuade other people, you convince them to do what you want them to do. It is meant to be a bit more overt—when you speak to the people that you are trying to convince, you will be able to influence them simply because you persuade them. Persuasion becomes a way for you to word things just right, phrasing your argument in convincing manners that will help you to get others to agree with you. Through the power of persuasion, you are able to get people to do whatever you could want them to. Think about how expert salespeople can convince someone to buy just about anything when they are good at their job—that is through sheer persuasion. Through utilizing the power of persuasion, they can tell people something and have that idea go through just right to influence the other party. This is a skill that just about everyone must master to some degree or another. Through mastering it, you are able to then begin to take control: You are able to persuade people into taking that skillset and utilize it for yourself. Through knowing what you are doing, you are able to ensure that what you say goes with ease. All you have to do is know a few key principles to follow along.

In this chapter, we will address two major points: The principles of persuasion, as well as rhetoric. These are two different methods that you are able to use to persuade other people to do whatever it is that you wanted them to do so that you are able to take control of a situation. If you are able to utilize these effectively, you are able to be on top of just about anything. You will be more likely to succeed and more likely to maintain that degree of confidence if you know how to utilize persuasion. The best leaders are often the most persuasive, and this is a skill that is necessary for many different jobs and career lines.

The Principles of Persuasion

First, we will consider the principles of persuasion. These are six key ways that you are able to phrase what you say or the situation that you are in so that you are able to be compelling to the people around you. When you know what you are doing, you will be able to utilize these skills in ways that will allow you to lead a situation naturally. Keep in mind that persuasion is a bit different from traditional manipulation—when you persuade someone, you are putting everything in front of them to see. You are showing them what you must do and how you must do it. You are teaching them the ways that they can begin to see the world so that they come to the conclusion that you want them to. This is much more indirect than true manipulation just due to the fact that usually, you are controlling the other person primarily through the way that you frame the situation. If you know what you are doing, you will be able to influence people with ease.

These work because, ultimately, they shift and influence the subconscious mind. They work by directly altering the way that you look at or treat other people in powerful ways. There are six different options that you are able to use: Reciprocity, consistency, social proof, authority, liking, and scarcity. Each of these will work in different ways to get that end result you are looking for.

Reciprocity

Reciprocity refers to the idea that when someone does something for you, you return the favor. This is the concept of giving and getting, and it helps people in social settings. When we engage in reciprocity, we feel like we must return things to people after we receive something from them in return. It helps to keep societies and family units running and drives people to work together to get the situations that are desired. If you are a car salesperson, for example, you probably have people coming in and out of your dealership constantly. You are able to help to get prospective clients to buy simply by making sure that you provide them with something in return first. If you wanted to, for example, you could give them a free coffee or give their children that they have with them lollipops. Such a small gesture actually goes a long way.

You are able to see this used in other contexts too—oftentimes, people get gifts given to them when they sign up for things, and they utilize that gift or that offer of a gift to encourage people. When they give you a gift, you feel more obligated or compelled to sign up as well. This is essential to being a social species and helps everyone. If you want to use this, then make sure that before you ask someone to do anything, you give them something first.

Consistency

There is a rule of human behavior that states that once someone starts saying yes to something, they will continue to say yes after. Think about it—when someone asks you to do something, and you agree, doing something a bit more doesn't seem as big of a deal. Think about it—imagine that someone asks you to toss something in the garbage as you walk past their desk. If that happens, then you would probably say yes: After all, it would be unreasonable for you to say no to that. Then, after you've said yes to that, you may find that they ask you to also pass them a pen as you come back. You agree to do that too because it isn't unreasonable to ask. From there, you might also be asked to pick something else up or glance over some paperwork. This is important to keep in mind for future use.

Imagine this—you are trying to get through some negotiations, but the other person is unreasonably stubborn. What are you supposed to do? The easiest answer is that you would simply utilize the idea of consistency in commitments to get them to agree to what you want. When you have to negotiate with someone who is clearly uninterested in negotiations, the best thing for you to do is to ask them to do something simple for you. You might ask them to pass that pen next to them because doing so forces them to move to open up their own body language, and once they agree to that, you are able to slowly get them to agree to other things as well.

Social proof

One of the main points that have been repeated throughout the entire book reiterated for importance is that we are social animals by nature. People love to be wanted and needed. We need to feel like we belong somewhere, even if that is just with our own friends and family. We want to feel like we are able to relate to people or like we are accepted. This is our drive to be social with others. It is also a common form of social proof that can be used as well. If you want to make sure that you are in control of a situation, then you are able to ensure that you get that social proof through making sure that you are laying on that peer pressure.

Effectively, if you are using social proof, you will be convincing the other person that they ought to do things a certain way because that is the way that everyone else does it as well. By doing so, you can make use of pointing out how other people do what you want them to do. You can show them that ultimately if they want to be like everyone else, that is what they will need to do. They will need to find a way to relate to everyone else just because of the fact that they will be doing different things. When you do this effectively, you will learn that you can do more. You will discover that you are more than capable of convincing people of just about anything.

Imagine, for example, you want someone to buy a specific item. You tell them that they should want to buy that item specifically because you know that their hero or their favorite athlete buys that item. This is precisely what you see done when you see advertisers using famous sponsors for their product—they want to rely on that social proof to sell their products for them.

Authority

Authority is a simple principle to understand—this principle dictates that when given a choice, you will always defer to a perceived authority. Imagine that your car just broke down. You might search for how to fix it online, but if your neighbor comes up to you and says, "Hey, I'm a mechanic, and I'm pretty sure this is what is wrong with your car," you are quite likely to believe them. Because they positioned themselves in that frame of being an authority figure, you are more likely to defer to them.

This can commonly be used in sales positions or in positions in which you want your authority to be taken seriously. Imagine, for example, that you want to get someone to listen to you. You might be a consulter for something, for example. You might want to consider putting up testaments to your achievements in the room around you. Maybe you have degrees and accolades all around, hanging on the walls. Perhaps you have an award from that time you won the award for the best service. By putting up these signs that you have done well, you assert yourself as an authority figure so that you can be certain that everything works according to plan. When you do this, you will realize that you are setting yourself up to be an authority to get that power over them. This is imperative— you must be able to accept and embrace that power for yourself. Assert why you should be in charge and do not back down from it. Make it clear that you deserve it.

Liking

Another simple principle to utilize is the idea of liking. This principle states that if you like something or someone, you are more likely to say yes when asked to do something. Think about it—you are much more likely to go out of your way to help a good friend or family member that you like than of someone that you dislike. This is imperative to keep in mind: You want to make sure that people who you like are taken care of, and that usually translates into helping them when they ask you to. This means, then, that if you want to get help from someone else, you want to make sure that they like you as well. You need a way to assert yourself as someone that is likable to them so that they will feel compelled to help you somehow. This can happen in all sorts of different ways, depending upon what you want to do and how you do it. However, there are three criteria to be well-liked by people:

1. You must be seen as human to the other person. This is especially important if you are attempting to get someone to help you that you do not yet know. You want to make sure that they see you as personalized. You might try putting up pictures of your family or say how you can relate to the other person. You could relate to their car, what they are wearing, or even if you have children around the same age as the other person. These simple acts can help you to be seen as a person to the individual that you are interacting with, and by doing so, you can help yourself as well.

2. You must then make them feel good about themselves when you talk to them. You want to encourage those good feelings because they will then associate you with those good feelings. However, you must be mindful of the way that you do so—you cannot come across as if you are trying to butter them up. You must come across as genuine. Make sure that whatever you compliment is something that you genuinely like, so you do not have to lie to them about something. This is the best way to be effective with how you engage with them.

3. Finally, you must cooperate with them. Make sure that whatever the two of you are doing is suddenly a team effort. You can make this happen in all sorts of different ways. Encourage them to see the situation as collaborative. Ask them to help you help them. This is a great way to make them relate to you and, therefore, like you more.

When you put those steps into place, you will be able to better influence them to like what is going on. It is highly effective in ensuring that they do want to help you out along the way, and if you can master how you do this, you can actually make great progress in getting them to be on your side.

Scarcity

Finally, the last principle of persuasion is that of scarcity. This simple principle tells you that there is more value when things are scarce than when they are plentiful. This makes perfect sense—if you want something that is hard to get, you will inherently value it higher than if it were easily acquired without much effort. This means that if you want to really get something from someone, you must ensure that you are on the right track. You must make sure that you choose out what you are doing and when you do it so that your time or your skills are scarce. You want to make them feel like they have to work to get what you are giving, or make them feel pressured.

This is precisely why so many salespeople will offer you a good deal and then put a short expiration on it. Perhaps you are trying to buy a house, and your realtor continually puts 24-hour limits on the offers—this is to pressure the individual to accept what you have offered up. If you want to be able to get a house, you want them to feel like your offer is not just sitting there idly for weeks at a time, tying up your money—you want that pressure there to encourage them to take it. Scarcity will work well to persuade people or push them toward a choice sooner rather than later, something that you may find that you really need as you continue forward.

Rhetoric and Persuasion

Beyond simple principles of persuasion, you should also recognize that persuasion can also be considered from a lens of rhetoric. This refers to the idea that your speech should also be persuasive. If you want to persuade others to do something, you must make sure that you do so the right way. This means making sure that you work through what you are doing and speak in certain ways. The best way to motivate people, then, is to use some sort of rhetorical appeal. In rhetoric, there are three appeals that a person can make: An appeal to character, an appeal to emotion, and an appeal to logic. Each works slightly differently and gets completely different results when you utilize them. All you have to do is know what you are doing.

Appeal to character

The appeal to character requires you to set yourself up as an authority figure of some sort. You want to find a way that you can frame yourself to be this authority so the other person feels like they must listen to you. It could be that you are experienced in what you are discussing. You could have gone through something that makes you uniquely qualified to talk about whatever you are discussing.

When you use this appeal, make sure that your discussion or speech to the other person focuses on what you have done that puts you in that position of being qualified to talk. You want to ensure that they see a reason to believe in you or what you are saying so that you are successfully able to discuss what is happening. This is oftentimes done through making a backstory that is highly compelling to the audience, or by explaining how you are capable of getting the results that you are looking for. By knowing what you are doing and making it happen, you can be certain that you will get what you want from the audience. They will be more likely to follow you if they feel that they have a good reason to.

Appeal to emotion

Appeals to emotion are a bit different—they are designed to make someone feel an emotion so that the emotion that is triggered can be used to influence the person. It could be that you add information through discussing an emotional event, or you try to point out something that happened when someone did not do what you wanted them to. Perhaps you say that the family that did not opt for the extra safety features on their car got into an accident, and everyone was seriously injured. Maybe you discuss how the last person to not follow your diet advice ended up with diabetes and getting a foot amputated. You want the stories that are used to evoke strong emotion because that strong emotion will then compel the behaviors that you are looking for from the person. You want them to feel the reasons that they should give you whatever you are looking for or asking for so that they do it.

Appeal to logic or reasoning

Finally, an appeal to logic is a form of persuasion that will throw logic, facts, and numbers at the individual in order to create an argument that is so compelling, the best thing that can be done is to accept it. These arguments, however, are rarely actually as logically sound as they are supposed to be. They are often skewed to try to get the individual to agree just to win the argument. Commonly, there will be a barrage of statistics that will be too overwhelming to parse through little by little, so the individual will simply choose to do as you have asked instead of trying to fight it or figure out what would work best for them. When people hear that there are factual reasons for them to follow what is being pushed, they are much more likely to agree just by default.

CHAPTER 9
Hypnosis

At this point, it is time to address the act of hypnosis as a form of influence over people. When you use hypnosis, you are capable of strongly influencing them through simply acting in certain ways. Hypnosis is not simply getting someone to go around clucking like a chicken—it is not waving a pendulum to get utter compliance. Rather, it is the act of getting someone into a state of gentle suggestiveness so that they are willing to accept your suggestions and act upon them. It is not closing off one's mind or shutting it down—it is actually a point of hyper-focusing. It is there to cause the mind to focus so intently on just one thing that it feels as if they are not all there. This is because their mind is stuck on whatever it is that they are focusing on.

It is not instantaneous, nor is it something that puts someone to sleep. In fact, they are actually going to be incredibly awake during these trance states. Hypnosis is defined as a trance-like state in which the individual is open to suggestions, relaxed, and heightened in imagination as well. There is a degree of hyper-focus and alertness that leads to ignoring just about everything in your surroundings, despite the fact that you will be completely conscious.

When you hypnotize someone else, you set them up so that they are entirely willing to accept your suggestions. You will feel or think whatever you are told. If you hypnotize someone and then tell them that they have a bag of lead on them so they cannot move, they will believe you, even if nothing is there. They will be entirely convinced that they cannot move, and they will remain there. When you encourage this state of mind, then, you are given direct access to the unconscious mind that you can use to control the rest of the thoughts that someone has.

Essentially, hypnosis works because of the fact that it will fast-track information straight to your unconscious mind. Remember, you are fully aware of what is in your consciousness, but not the unconscious. If you are trying to influence someone to feel like they must do something, then you want to do so through getting to their unconscious in the first place. You want to suggest things to it so that they will be more willing to act them out in the first place. This means that you are fully expecting the individual to relax into a state where anything that you say is going to naturally be absorbed into the mind. You want them to figure out how they can talk to you in a way that will allow for this.

As you get into that state of suggestibility, you get to a point in which you are not inhibited by your conscious thought. Your conscious mind is highly logical—it is the part of your mind that is there to influence you or make you feel like you are inhibited. It is the part of your mind that tells you that dancing on top of that ledge on top of a cliff is a dangerous idea and that you should probably avoid doing so. When you hypnotize someone, however, you can suggest that they should dance on that ledge, they probably feel like it is a good idea. They will absorb those thoughts or suggestions right into their subconscious, and as a result, they will fall for exactly what you have suggested from them. If you do this the wrong way, you will find that you fail.

While many people doubt that hypnosis is a real thing, it has been backed by science on more than one occasion. The body's vital signs do not really change much during the state of hypnosis, but it is the case that the brain's activity does change notably and significantly during these states. It has been found through electroencephalographs (EEGs) that during hypnosis, wave frequency is lowered. This is what commonly is also found during dreaming states in terms of brain activity. At the same time, the higher frequency waves, usually associated with alertness, are dropped. This allows for the support that the conscious mind is actively subdued during periods of hypnosis to allow for the subconscious mind to be so accessible.

There have also been studies done under hypnosis that show that activity is reduced within the left hemisphere's cerebral cortex. It is then increased on the right side, which is the part of the brain that rules imagination and creativity. By inhibiting activity in the left hemisphere, the conscious mind's logical nature is suppressed, while the increase of activity on the right side implies that there are more creative aspects focused upon.

All of this implies that there is a very real phenomenon known as hypnosis, and it absolutely is effective in its own ways. Through being able to understand this process effectively, you can then start to utilize it as well. Now, let's consider a few different types of hypnosis to begin understanding the process of using it.

Hypnotizing Through Speech

First, let's consider hypnosis through speech. When you want to hypnotize someone without them catching on, you can usually do so through the word choice that you utilize. Using words that will heavily imply relaxation can often work well for this, much like what you would expect with NLP methods of influence on people. If you want to trigger that state of influence in someone, you must make sure that you lead with the right kind of language that will then encourage those feelings or thoughts that you want them to utilize.

In hypnosis, you must trigger a state of relaxation, and with this, you will start encouraging it through progressive relaxation and imagery. Through utilizing your voice instead of tools, you can usually encourage calmness. If you have ever listened to a guided meditation that has been narrated before, you have been hypnotized by the gentle nature of speech that you heard. The best way to get it to work is to use a low and soothing voice, much like if you were trying to shush and lull a baby to sleep. If you can make this happen the right way, you can then encourage the individual to feel much more relaxed.

As you speak, you must command their absolute attention. You must make sure that they are listening to you so you can get them to follow along into that suggestive state. As you continue to speak, you must suggest relaxing. This can be done by discussing just how calming it would be to do something. Maybe you mention softly that it is so peaceful to watch those apple blossoms blow off of the apple tree in your front yard, watching them fall one by one down the path. Maybe you talk about the gentle nature of the river as it flows downstream or the quiet softness of falling snow. As you slowly and calmly speak, you lull the other person into a state of relaxation as well. Through doing so, willing minds will then naturally start to relax as well. You will trigger that trance-like state that you are looking for, and in that state, you can then influence them to get them to do whatever it is that you were looking for from them.

Hypnotizing With Movements

When you want to hypnotize someone through movements, you are doing something similar to when you are speaking. However, this time, you are drawing upon your ability to mirror someone else, and then you are slowly easing them into following your own repetitive movements with ease. You want them to follow along so that you can be certain that they are on the same page as you and so that they will naturally follow your actions as well. Think about how when you rock an infant to sleep, they are quickly soothed by the motion, and how it is possible for you to do the same to yourself. How many people fall asleep in rocking chairs or on the long car ride home when they are a passenger? It can be easy to fall asleep if you do not have anything keeping you from doing so.

Movements can be incredibly relaxing to help you ease into that state of mind in which you can influence other people. All you have to do is make sure that as you move, you will be able to tap into what you want. You might be able to gently sway as you discuss something with someone else, encouraging them to do the same. This will then cause them to relax more, and as they begin to relax more, they will naturally follow along with what you ask of them. They will start feeling much more inclined to do what you want as you ask them to do something.

Hypnotizing Through Repetitive Sounds

Finally, you can also induce a state of hypnosis through a droning voice that is quite repetitive as well. Think back to your time in school. Did you ever feel like you were falling asleep just by listening to what other people around you were saying? This is caused by hypnosis—or at least, a similar premise. Though your teacher may not have intentionally tried to hypnotize you, they did so through their droning, repetitive voice that did not vary much. This, done without any fluctuations at all in pitch, voice, or speed, can be mind-numbing, and as a result, it leads to people who are not really paying much attention. It triggers that desire to daydream or that lack of attention to what is going on around them. This is a great way for you to take control of someone else without them ever being aware of it.

This is a bit harder to do naturally because if you talk with a flat drone, most people will question you. However, if you know what you are doing, you can bore the mind of the other person into submission, allowing you to start adding in what you want them to do into your script after a while. This is actually a common method that is used in indoctrinating people into cults. You make it a point to drone on as much as possible to control the other person, and as a result, you capture their minds and their efforts. This is highly useful if you know what you are doing.

CHAPTER 10
Reverse Psychology

When we were in school, we all tried out reverse psychology at one point or another. Reverse psychology becomes this exciting thing for people when they realize that it often works far better than most people expect it to—when you are exposed to reverse psychology, you often feel like you are caught up in something that forces you to do something. It is something that happens mostly toward children, but if done well, it can actually utilize the psychological phenomenon known as reactance.

Reactance is the negative reaction to trying to be persuaded. It is that defiant attitude that people often take when someone tries to get them to do something or that attitude that tells the other person that they have no choice but to do something or attempt something. Through reactance, you can run into all sorts of problems. You want to make sure that you can limit this—but sometimes, you can use it to your advantage if you know how to push it a bit further. You would simply want to make sure that you are a step ahead of the other person. If you know, for example, that someone is quite reactive or volatile when you try to get them to do something, you might want to use that to your advantage. This could be, for example, trying to tap into someone's resistant nature to give indirect orders.

For the vast majority of people, direct orders are good enough. However, there are many people out there that require this indirect approach to sort of guide them into that reaction that you are looking for. This is somewhat paradoxical—the resistant people fall for this sort of manipulation—but it is something that you should be well aware of.

The idea here is that some people are simply contrarian: When they are told not to do something, they feel that deep desire to do it anyway. They find that they really want to do it instead of giving in to it. They want to find a way for themselves to avoid doing what they were told what to do. Because of this, if you know that someone is likely to respond like this, all you have to do is make it a point to understand the impulse. You simply tell them to do the opposite of what you want from them, and they, because of their contrarian nature, do the opposite. Of course, they do exactly what you want when you encourage this, and you get your way after all.

However, not everyone is going to fit into this. You will need to be mindful of how you utilize this.

Reverse psychology is one of those things that work in many ways that might sound like they do not make much sense at first but are actually highly effective. If you want to make sure that you are getting that reaction from people that you want, you will need to ensure that you also understand what they do and when they do it. You must make sure that you figure out what you want from them, and what the opposite of this is as well.

Using Reverse Psychology

If you want to use reverse psychology, you need to make sure that you approach the person the right way. First, are they someone that is going to respond to reverse psychology? Not everyone will—it takes a certain kind of contrarian to give in to reverse psychology so you can utilize it yourself. It takes a certain kind of contrarian for you to ensure that everyone around you is going to behave a certain way when you suggest something. Thankfully, there are some tips and tricks that can help you to tap into this use of reverse psychology for those who either hate being bossed around or for the overconfident people who believe that they have nothing to worry about.

Challenge the other person

First, you could consider challenging the other person to do something when you want the opposite. Challenge them while insisting that they cannot do what you want from them. You could tell them that there is no way that they can successfully do what you want from them. Or, you could tell them that they have no hope of getting what you want. This will then trigger them to feel compelled to prove you wrong. Their drive to prove you wrong will be enough for you to get that result that you were looking for.

Remain calm

Of course, when you are using reverse psychology, you should also remain calm at all times. This is necessary, so they feel like they are spiraling out of control. If you can encourage this the right way, you can get that success that you were looking for. The more that you do this, the more likely that you are to get that success the right way. This is especially important if you use reverse psychology on children—they need that stability and that calm attitude from you to show them that they can trust what is happening or that they are comfortable.

Make them think they chose it

The key goal here is to lead them to the action that you want while also making them think that they brought themselves there willingly. That is the real key here—those who fall for reverse psychology are those that are much less likely to fall for it otherwise if they do not wholeheartedly believe that they chose out what they are doing or how they are doing it. This means that you must find a way to make it their own idea before they insist on anything else.

Remember your goal

As you use this form of influence on the other person, make sure that you do not lose sight of your real goal. Make sure that you cling to that idea of success and what it will be. You must ensure that you are on the right page and that you continue to work toward what you wanted. This is imperative: You want to ensure that you can get it met, after all.

Say the opposite of what you want

When you utilize reverse psychology, everything is the opposite of what you want. You must make it clear to them that you want something that is contrary to what you actually want because that is what will trigger them to rebel- than getting you exactly what you wanted in the first place. You want to do this in an even tone. Do not let them think that you are lying, or they are going to see right through your attempts to control them in this way.

CHAPTER 11
Brainwashing

A very specific form of manipulation is known as brainwashing. This is something that only happens in very specific situations and must be deliberate. The process of brainwashing is unorthodox and largely illegal—but it is something that is possible to do. Through brainwashing, you are able to effectively convince someone to take an entirely new perspective on the world. You are effectively convincing them that they are someone new, building them a brand new identity that you control and influence. This is effectively just thought reform—it can be seen in all sorts of different contexts.

First, it is important to note that the information that you see here in front of you comes from an understanding of an event that happened to several American prisoners that were held during the Korean War. They were kept in camps and then brainwashed into believing that they were using germ warfare and that they must pledge their allegiance to the idea of communism and Korea. During this time, these prisoners had their entire minds erased. They were told to forget and relinquish their past lives and become someone new.

This is a form of mind control that works to completely rewrite the thoughts of someone else through forcefully breaking them down into someone that you can control. It is designed to inflict harm and distress to the point that they relinquish their past lives and choose to be whatever it is that you want them to be out of self-preservation and as you go through the steps involved, you will see how this new persona is developed, created and crafted entirely by captors that want nothing more than to control the individual and make them who they want.

Brainwashing works because the person that does the brainwashing in the first place gets complete control over the target. The person that is brainwashed has no choice but to obey or be harmed. Over time, the brainwasher is then able to completely dismantle that personality, little by little, until the new one is crafted to the individual's liking. The one that was brainwashed then adopts that new personality in hopes of remaining safe long-term.

How Brainwashing Works

Brainwashing is something that takes place over ten distinct steps that come together and create that final instance in which people are stuck with whatever happens. It works through brutally dismantling everything that the individual knows, discarding those identities and allegiances until only the desired person is left behind for them.

Assault on identity

This first step is designed to create complete destruction of the self. It is meant to destroy one's identity, little by little. This is done by telling someone that everything they thought that they knew was false. There are common questions about one's identity here, and each time, they are then disregarded. Perhaps their name is asked, and they are told that they are wrong, or if they say they have family, they are told that is a lie. The context for this step is that the attacker must deny everything that the individual says about themselves. Everything is deemed to be false when they try to assert themselves, and as a result, they feel confused. This should happen in particular through to the point of exhaustion to be fully effective. When the individual is thoroughly exhausted or vulnerable, often through sleep deprivation and starvation to create that vulnerability, they will give in, and slowly, their own understanding of who they are as an individual is entirely dismantled.

Guilt

Next comes guilt. With this stage, the individual is made to feel guilty. They are told that everything is their fault, and the guilt is often tied specifically to their identity. By assigning guilt as a defining factor of who someone is, there is that additional control over them. It allows for that full claiming of who they are and what they do. It allows for the brainwasher to step in and assert that they must reject everything. The idea here is that an identity that is wrapped up in guilt is easier to give up than one wrapped in positivity.

Self-betrayal

The third is self-betrayal. This is the stage in which the agent, the one doing the brainwashing, is able to get the target to agree with the assertions and attempt to assign guilt. This is to cause the individual to recognize that they were bad so that they can let go of who they were before. They need to feel like their choices were wrong so that they can let them go.

Breaking point

The breaking point comes after the betrayal of the self. It is the point at which the individual gives up—they just cannot do it any longer. They may have a complete nervous breakdown at this stage, crying and depressed, or even feel like they must commit suicide or harm themselves.

Leniency

However, when everything seems lost, and hope is abandoned, the brainwasher steps in to offer just a smidge of kindness—a touch of leniency that is meant to help. At the moment, when everything is bleak, this tiny act of kindness becomes enough to allow for that brainwashing to work entirely. You will see that someone may give you a sip of water, or they might also make a move to change how they talk. They might offer a cigarette or a bit of extra food. This makes the individual feel like they are in debt.

Releasing guilt

After that point of kindness, the individual often feels a desire to confess to release the guilt that they have. They feel like there is hope—but to get that hope back, they must reject everything that they have clung to just a bit more. They must make sure that they are able to get what they want and to get it, they let go of everything. Their will to live makes them feel like the only way to stay safe is if they confess.

Channeling guilt

At this point, they assume that they were the problem all along. They assume that all problems were their own doing and that if they want them fixed, they will have to do something about it. They will need to channel that guilt so that they can begin to release it. Often, this is done by wrapping their guilt around their identity and then choosing to start rejecting it.

Progress toward harmony

Next comes the desire to begin moving toward salvation or the goodness that they think that they can get if they denounce who they were before. This progression toward harmony involves them choosing to let go of what they thought they were and accepting the ideas from their captors or brainwashers. They start to recognize that through compliance and assimilation, they can escape the abuse. To make this happen, they start complying with assimilation demands. They take on that reliable, new identity at the urging of their brainwashers.

Final confession

Finally, it all ends when the new life is adopted completely. All old beliefs are rejected, and instead, the individual pledges allegiance to that brand new life and identity. This usually involves some sort of ceremony that allows them to take on that identity in a crowd. At this point, they are recognized as being fully assimilated and are allowed to interact with other people, who may or may not accept them.

CHAPTER 12
Seduction

Have you ever wished that you could seduce someone else? It is something that some people wish that they could do on a whim— maybe they see someone that they are attracted to. Perhaps they feel like they must do it if they want to be in a relationship. Maybe they just want a one-night-stand. No matter what, however, seduction is something that can be mastered relatively easily. If you know what you are doing and you are ruthless enough to not care about this idea of trying to get someone to want you, then you can utilize seduction with ease. You just have to know what you are getting yourself into.

This is a skill that is perfect if it is not yet time to settle down, but you could really use a night or two of some fun with someone new. If someone catches your eye at the bar, you might want to try to win them over, and the easiest way to do so is through seduction. If you feel like you really want someone to want you, you need to trigger it if it is not an instantaneous occurrence. Most of the time, attraction happens almost immediately, so if you do not notice it right off the bat when you get started in an interaction, then you might want to find a way to make it happen otherwise.

First of all, let's identify the fact that anyone can seduce someone else—male or female; you are capable of influencing someone in this manner if you know what you are doing. If you know how to talk to them or what they might want, you can encourage them to feel like they must actually want you after all. You just have to tap into those feelings and make them happen for yourself. If you can do that, you will be successful here.

In this chapter, we have a few key points to address. First, we will take some time to work out a proper definition of seduction. Then, we will look at how you can choose the right target. After all, not all people can be swayed in the same ways, and if you do not know what you are doing, you might pick out the wrong person—which could very quickly backfire. Then, you must figure out what it is that you can do to begin to seduce other people. By working through all three of these topics, you should be prepared to use it if you choose to do so.

What Is Seduction?

Before we begin, let's touch upon the idea of seduction. Though it is commonly believed to be morally corrupt or the act of leading someone astray, it is not exactly just that. It is a bit more. Though contextually, it sounds like you are simply trying to hurt someone with how you engage with them, there is more to it. It is not inherently corruptive, though it absolutely can be if you choose to target someone that is already in a relationship.

What it is, however, is a way to sway someone to do something that they may not have thought they would do initially. You could seduce someone into being attracted to you. It could be getting someone else to want to pursue you. It could also be attempting to convince them to go on a date with you. However, keep in mind that there is a difference between seduction, which is encouraging them to consent to do what you want, and forcing your will upon someone else. Seduction is a way in which you pursue someone else into making them consent without trying to coerce them. It is important to remember that your seduction should not go past that idea of consent and if you get a clear and resounding no, then you must respect that.

Choosing a Target

Seduction is a bit tricky to manage—the most important step of all is making sure that the person that you are trying to seduce is a proper target. You must make sure that you are choosing someone that is open to your advances, or at the very least, is not entirely shut down by them. You want to make sure that they are going to be willing. They need to *want* to be seduced. If they do not seem like they are very willing or receptive, there is probably a reason for it, and you should not attempt to coerce them into it. Remember, coercion is not seduction—you must mind the line to avoid falling into that trap. You need to bear in mind that seduction is something more nuanced.

To be open for seduction, consider three key points: Receptiveness, unhappiness, and alluring or attractiveness. Your idea target will hit all three of these points—they will be interested in being seduced for one reason or another, and this often overlaps with that unhappiness that comes with a desire for more. When you see this, you usually find someone at the end of a relationship or wishing that they were able to get out of the relationship and find someone new. There is something about their current relationship that is inherently unsatisfying, and when you show up, you represent that ability to get more. Finally, they must be attractive to you somehow, so you actually feel like you want to pursue them.

If your target does not fit all three of these points, then someone is going to end up unhappy. Now, you might enjoy the thrill of the chase in pursuing someone, but if you are not actually attracted to them, you are not going to be very happy with the end result either way. You are not going to want to be with them if you do not like them or find that you are entirely turned off by them. Because of this, you must consider all points. Once you do that, you can start seducing.

Using Seduction

When it comes to seducing, there are all sorts of different techniques that you can use based upon the target that you have chosen and just how receptive or not receptive that you think that they will be. How likely do you think that they are to want to do something? Let's go over several seductive strategies—you can choose out the ones that work the best for you. Remember, this is a sort of trial and error situation—it will take time and effort to figure out what works well for different people, and with every new target that you seduce, you will see that there are very different results that you can get.

Mixed signals

When you send mixed signals to someone else, you are effectively attempting to make yourself stand out or be memorable. You are essentially working to make yourself interesting—you send these mixed signals that make you paradoxical, which is inherently intriguing just by virtue of being a paradox. You will naturally get people's attention when you appear to be two contradictory things. You will be exciting, and that draws people into you. Through making it a point to show several different kinds of qualities, some of which may be quite contradictory, you start to get attention directed right toward yourself.

In doing this, you make yourself seem interesting one way or another. Think about the person that you are targeting and figure out what you think they would like. Are they talking to all of the "bad boys" at the bar? Make yourself seem tougher, but then just as quickly, also show a tender side. Maybe someone drops something, and you stop to give it to them, or you offer your prime seat at the bar to an older gentleman who came in to watch the game. By doing something that is sympathetic and kind, you display that you are not all bad and show them that they can, and they will be able to expect you to be kinder in many different situations. This works well and shows depth in your personality as well—something that many people often forget all about.

Make yourself desirable

You should also work to make sure that you come across as desirable as well. Remember that principle of scarcity? Time to make use of it—it is time to appeal to the idea that you look like you are scarce by getting the attention of other people. By making the individual that you are interested in believe that you are in demand with other people, you are much more likely to get them to come toward you quickly. They will want to ensure that they are getting those results that they are looking for. Overall, if other people find you fascinating or interesting, you must be worthy, and people will start to flock to you as well.

Make the other person feel anxious

Remember, one of the best things that you can play up during this whole process is anxiety. This is important—you want to remind the other person of just how unhappy they are, so they start to see you as an option to finding the solution to the unhappiness that you have in the first place. The more that you do this, the more likely that you are to get that unhappiness all settled and resolved. You effectively want them to feel anxious in covert ways. You want them to be unaware of what is happening so you can actually make it work for you in the first place. You want to do this all as covertly as possible as well—you don't want them to be aware of what you are doing or how you are actively attempting to pursue them.

Adapt to their preferences

If you are trying to seduce someone, then you must become whatever it is that they want from you. If they want you to be someone that is going to be kinder, then do that. If they seem to want those tough guys, then be that as well. You want to work to create an artificial image of yourself in the other person's mind effectively. You want them to feel like they want you at all costs. You want them to feel like you are highly desirable or like they will not get you if they do not know what they are doing. By making sure that you show them what they want to see, you can actually win them over quicker.

Lay on the sweet talk

People do not listen very well when they do not hear what they want to hear. This means that if you want someone's attention, you want to tell them what they do want to hear. The more that you can do that, the more likely that you are to actually get them to look to you. They will see that you are saying what they want to hear, and they will then pay closer attention. Why wouldn't they? Sweet talk them—inflate their egos a bit. Make them feel good, so they like you more. This will help you to win them over and get that result that you want. You will trigger them to feel compelled to follow along with what you want.

Tempt them

When you tempt them, you will show them what they could have instead of what they currently do. You are showing them that a slight glimpse through the fence that shows them that the grass is greener—but by doing so in the way that you do, you are making them want to follow you. Let them see a bit of what things could be like if they chose you. Maybe flirt with them. Build that sexual tension. Create that spark of attraction and chemistry that is undeniable for them—they will want to pursue it. That little glimpse can become all-consuming and drive them to want to be around you more. If you play your cards just right, you will be able to get them to want you.

Parent your target

This might seem somewhat counterintuitive but consider for a moment that for most people, they felt the safest as a child when they were with their parents. People look back fondly to their childhoods when they were sheltered, safe, and free to do what they wanted when they wanted it, and because of that, you can actually start to trigger those happy feelings and those fond moments of being taken care of just by being careful around the person that you want to attract. If you know what you are doing, you can start to care for them, little by little. Suggest that they put on a jacket because it is cold. Offer to get something for them. Keep them safe. By being concerned for their wellbeing, you can make them feel more secure with you, and that will also trigger them to be more interested in you as well.

Make insinuations

When you insinuate something, you say something without having to say the words, implying it through indirect language that you use to seduce them. You are trying to create that degree of uncertainty that will help you to take control of the situation that you are in to properly lead the other person. If you know what you are doing, you can get them to want to follow you and what you are doing and saying.

Create suspense

By creating a suspenseful feeling, you will effectively encourage them to become interested in you. Because they cannot tell what will come next or what you will do, you become interesting to them. They decide that they want to pursue you just because they are unsure of what to expect, and they do not know how to deal with the situation or what they should be doing. By carefully fabricating situations in which the suspense can be maintained, you can keep your target interested in you for far longer than you probably realized you could. This is perfect for you if you are unsure of what you will be doing long-term in that relationship.

Play the victim

Though it can seem counterintuitive, playing the victim will actually help you immensely here—it will help you to properly recognize that point in which you are in control of a situation. When you play the victim the right way, you can follow that line between showing that you are manipulating so much that they can see it right in front of them and being too light on trying to influence them. You want to make it so that they think they are superior, and you are the one that is vulnerable. By making yourself the vulnerable one, you make it so that they believe that you are not a threat. This will grant you that power to seduce them longer term.

Balance the highs and lows

Another point to consider is making sure that you are not too nice. You need to balance out the highs and the lows to maintain that type of appearance that you want. Kindness and niceness are great in a relationship, but if you are just seducing someone, you need to recognize that they are also boring because they are safer. You want to make sure that you are not making yourself boring—instead, work to ensure that you appear to be interesting. Make lows that make the high points in your relationship or interactions seem better. Consider this for a moment: In a relationship, if the neutral state is you simply getting along and aiming to please, it can be quite boring to be there with someone else. However, when you add in those artificial lows, the neutral and high points of your interactions become that much more compelling for you instead. Make them feel guilty sometimes or insecure sometimes so that when you make them feel special, it is even more special than it would have been.

CHAPTER 13
Spotting Manipulation

Finally, the last chapter in this book is all about figuring out where the manipulation lies. Though you now know how to influence people in many different ways, it is time to recognize that there is more to it than meets the eye. When you want to manipulate someone else, you must make it a point to understand their own vulnerabilities, but what about your own? When it comes to being able to navigate through the world, you must also be able to spot manipulation so that you can control it yourself as well. You must be able to protect yourself from the manipulative attempts all around you—you need to find ways that you can spot it before it ever becomes a problem for you.

Thankfully, or not so thankfully, manipulation is something that is relatively easy to spot if you know what you are looking for and if you can keep your attention where it needs to be. By learning the signs of manipulation, you can spot it before it happens to you. Remember, manipulation can happen in just about any context. It could occur in a relationship, in a family situation, or otherwise. It could happen at work, or it could be something that only happens with a certain friend. No matter when or where it happens, it is important to note that being manipulated is not fun. It is not typically a good feeling to realize that other people have been trying to control you, and you will want to try to do something to prevent it, if at all possible. If you are trying to spot manipulation in your own life, try to keep an eye out for these various signs that we are going to be going over—they will help you to spot when there is a problem or if you need to do something else to prevent it.

Constant Accusations

When someone is manipulating you, they will constantly accuse you of things. They will make you feel like you are being controlled or like you have to give in to them. Their accusations leave you wondering what is going on and leave you feeling entirely trapped in the situation that you are in. They may accuse you of lying or cheating even when you are not, and they actually are. This is a common projection method that will happen.

Additionally, you might feel like you have to accuse the manipulator as well because not everything seems quite right. You cannot put your finger on it, but things are going wrong, and you blame them for it—something that they then vehemently deny. They do not take fault at all.

Mind Games

Mind games happen regularly when you are in the presence of a manipulator. Just consider the context of this entire book—much of it involved playing mind games to control the other party. If you feel like you are constantly being controlled, it is time to consider that the relationship that you have with the individual is actually manipulative. Keep in mind, however, that they will not concede defeat. They will not admit when they are at fault because they want to keep you easy to control and docile, and that is often done through sheer instability. They want you to feel like you are unstable so they can maintain control over the situation.

Your Items Keep Getting Damaged

If you find that your objects are constantly getting damaged, usually much more often than the other person's objects, then there is a chance that there is actually something more going on here. Often, manipulators will damage things that will cause feelings of distress or upset solely because they want that control. Remember, negative emotions are one of the biggest weaknesses that you can get from someone. This is meant to make you upset so you can be controlled more.

The Other Party Is Jealous

Jealousy often happens in the relationship, and often, the manipulator will also attempt to get it installed in the relationship to take control as well. They want you to feel like you are jealous so they can wield that jealousy as a tool for themselves. If you voice a complaint, they will simply say that you are jealous and that they can do what they want. Think about how a manipulator might flirt with someone in front of their partner and, when confronted, say that the other party was simply too jealous and that they should not have been so concerned.

The Other Party Is Always a Victim

If you notice that the other party is always a victim when you are in a relationship, this is often an attempt to influence or manipulate the other party. It is done for that degree of control and is entirely intentional. By being the victim, the individual can then trigger guilt in you so that you feel much more likely to give them what they want. They want you to feel guilty so that they can avoid the blame while still maintaining that control over the situation. If you want to avoid being manipulated, then you must make sure that you spot the victims and weed them out of your life.

You Are Rushed Into Choices

If you feel like you are constantly being rushed into decisions, whether you should be or not, there is a real chance that you are being manipulated. This is done, so you do not have the time to think things through. If you had that time to think, then you might make a rational choice that would not represent what the manipulator wants. Instead, they decide to make the choices for you. They choose to push you to choose quickly, so they get to keep that control longer-term.

There Are Inconsistencies

If your entire relationship is defined by constant inconsistencies in actions and words, it is quite possibly manipulative. Manipulators are experts at saying things that they know the other party wants to hear solely because they want the other party to give in to them. They want to get the other party to do whatever they want, so they tell them something, only to renege on it later. This is common— they are betting on your complacency after you agree to do something, and they do not want to deal with it. If you know what you are doing, however, you can prevent this from becoming too problematic for yourself. You can stop the inconsistencies when you realize that they are there.

Everything Is a Negotiation

If everything that you do in your relationship is fraught with negotiation, there is a good chance that you are being manipulated into doing things for the other person. This is there to allow for the manipulator to get what they want while making the other party feel like they have a say when they really did not. They will make sure that they come out on top every single time while also making the victim feel like they gained something in the entire situation, even if there was nothing to gain in the first place.

Words Are Distorted

If you notice that what you say is constantly being taken out of context, then you are being manipulated. The best manipulators are able to take what someone said and spin it around so that the meaning they spin is the opposite of what was intended. This is done so they can then emotionally blackmail the other party into admitting their faults so they can take and maintain control over the situation. Through doing this little by little, they can ensure that they get to take over everything without much of a problem or battle.

You Constantly Feel Upset Around One Person

If you notice that you are only upset when you are around one person, or if your emotions are always frazzled after interactions with just one person, there is probably a good reason for that and that good reason is probably that you are being influenced in some significant way that you should consider fixing. If you constantly find yourself upset, look at the person that is causing those feelings. Why do they trigger them? If you really think about it, they are probably manipulating you.

You Feel a Strong Sense of Obligation for Someone

Likewise, if you feel an unnaturally strong sense of obligation toward someone that you cannot really explain, there is a good chance that you feel that due to some degree of manipulation that you will need to offset. If you know what you are doing, you should be able to prevent it. Spot the reason for the obligation. It is likely to be manipulative in nature, and when you spot it, you can then prevent it from controlling you.

You Feel Like You Have Changed

Finally, if you feel like you have changed more than makes sense considering the situation that you are in, it is time for you to start piecing together why. Figure out what it is that is causing these problems. Figure out why it is that you feel the way that you do, then make sure that you can influence or control it. Make sure that you figure out what you can do to stop it. Usually, that means that you will have to cut off the manipulator so you can protect yourself.

CONCLUSION

Thank you for making it through to the end of *Manipulation Techniques*. Let's hope it was informative and able to provide you with all of the tools you need to achieve your goals, whatever they may be.

At this point, you understand now what it is to influence other people. You have discovered the art of being able to directly influence and take charge of people so that you can assert what you want when you want it. You have now seen several different methods that you can use to influence other people, and because of that, you have now discovered what it will take for you to maintain that control long term. If you want to make sure that you can control those people around you, you will need to put these different tools to the test so that you can take charge where you need it. Remember, you now have all the power—all the cards in your hands.

As you read through this book, you were guided through several key ways that you could start to change the way that people acted, and it all began with a thought. It all began with being able to change that one individual thought so you could watch the feelings and behaviors follow along. By changing one thought, you can create an entirely different feeling. By changing one feeling, you can create a dramatically different behavior from what you may have initially expected. Because of this, you want to consider the different ways that people engage with each other. You want to consider that ultimately, we all behave differently. We all engage differently. We all act differently, and it all starts with the thought. From here, it is time for you to decide what you will do with your newfound knowledge. Are you going to make use of it for yourself? Are you going to influence yourself and how you engage with people? Are you going to control other people instead? Are you going to make sure that you come out on top, no matter what happens next? No matter where you decide that you are going next, one thing is for sure: You have the power. You can choose where it will be.

Remember, your power is one that you must use responsibly. You must choose how you wish to proceed now that you have this information for yourself. If you choose to use it for your own benefit, then you must also be ready to take responsibility for the actions as well. If the results are worth it to you, then what you do is your own choice. Remember to keep that in mind and also recognize how your actions will influence those around you at the same time. Make sure that you take the time to really recognize the ways that people around you engage. Take the time to consider how different people will interact with each other. Make sure that you are confident about your behaviors. Not all manipulation or influence is inherently bad—it has its own place sometimes, and sometimes it makes perfect sense to use it. However, that is something that you must work out over time. That is something for you to figure out on your own terms.

Nevertheless, you now have the information that you will need. Thank you for taking the time to read through this book. Thank you for considering everything that you know now about manipulation. Hopefully, you are ready to take the information out with you into the world to do the best possible things that you can do, and hopefully, as you do navigate, you make good choices.

Now, it is time for you to head out into the world and make use of this information. Hopefully, you feel a bit better with it in mind so you can use it if necessary. And finally, please consider taking the time to leave a review if you found that the information that you read in this book was useful. If it benefitted you, please let us know how. Your feedback is something that is always greatly appreciated and provides plenty to help ensure that future books work just as well as this one! And, if there are any suggestions that you have or if there is anything that you wish this book had covered, please consider leaving that behind in your review as well. Any feedback that you provide will make the next book even better than this one! Thank you once more, and good luck out there with this information! Hopefully, you are able to succeed in everything that you set out to do and more!

DESCRIPTION

Are you interested in being able to manipulate others? Have you wondered what you could do if you wanted to control the other people in your life? If so, then keep reading... This book could be exactly what you are looking for. When it comes to being able to influence and control the minds of other people, you want to ensure that you know what you are doing.

Remember, not all manipulation is bad. Manipulation is simply to mold someone—to make them do something through the power of your own influence. When you influence someone else through manipulation, you covertly pull strings to get them to do whatever it is that you needed from them. You can frame something a certain way, or you behave a certain way as well. You could choose to talk to someone to convince them to change up their thought processes, or you could persuade them to take your side by utilizing the principles of persuasion. One thing is for sure; however—there are many, many different options that you can use to make people believe whatever it is that you want.

Through developing the right way to approach the situation, you can put yourself in that position to help yourself. If you wanted to do so, you could make it happen yourself. When you read through this book, you will learn precisely how to influence and control the people around you. As you develop this skill, you develop the ability that you will need to keep in mind if you want to control other people. From emotional manipulation to persuasion and brainwashing or mind control, you can develop the ability to learn these different skills so you can be successful at influencing other people. You can expect to see:

- An understanding of what manipulation is and how it works
- Why the subconscious mind is key in using these techniques
- How you can begin to manipulate others
- Using emotional manipulation on other people to get them to do what you want when you want it
- Using mind control on other people and how it works
- Using NLP on other people, as well as several different methods that you can use
- Discovering the power of body language and how it can influence other people with just simple changes to how you stand about

- Developing the ability to utilize the principles of persuasion to control other people with your words, convincing them to trust your judgment
- Learning how to hypnotize people with ease so you can speak directly to their subconscious minds
- Discovering the power of reverse psychology and when and how it works
- Working on how to brainwash other people and how it works
- Developing the ability to use seduction
- Learning how to spot manipulation before it happens to you
- *AND MORE*

As you read through this book, you can learn everything you will need to know to control other people and how you can protect yourself as well. If you are ready to take control so you can be in charge, then you are in the right place—let's get started to see what you need to do. All you have to do is scroll up and click on BUY NOW today to get started!